WORDMAN

WORDMAN
A Writer on Writing

P.F. Kluge

A Peace Corps Writers Book —
an imprint of Peace Corps Worldwide

Published in the United States of America by
Peace Corps Writers of Oakland, California.

For more information, contact peacecorpsworldwide@gmail.com

Peace Corps Writers and the Peace Corps Writers colophon are
trademarks of PeaceCorpsWorldwide.org

Cover photo and author portrait by Floyd K. Takeuchi
Book design by Jerry Kelly

ISBN-13: 978-1-880977-43-9
Library of Congress Control Number: 2024900266
First Edition, January 2024

Also by P.F. Kluge

Fiction
The Williamson Turn
Master Blaster
A Call from Jersey
Gone Tomorrow
Final Exam
Biggest Elvis
MacArthur's Ghost
Season for War
Eddie and the Cruisers
The Day That I Die

Nonfiction
Keepers: Home & Away
Alma Mater: A College Homecoming
The Edge of Paradise: America in Micronesia

Essays
God the Disc Jockey
Breakfast in Ohio
Saipan: From Then to Now
My Private Germany
Day By Day
Remembering Saipan
The File Cabinet
Palau: The Age of Barbecue

Films
Dog Day Afternoon
Eddie and the Cruisers
Eddie and the Cruisers II

DEDICATION

For Matt Voorhees and George Stone, the Radler Gang,
with whom friendship and adventure have taken us to
Bali, Austria, Singapore, Prague, Morocco, Malacca,
Kaui, Germany…

And for my parents, who encouraged me, but didn't live
to see the stack of books with *Kluge* on the spine.

MY THANKS

This book would not have been possible without the support of my wife Pamela Hollie and friends like Floyd Takeuchi, who knows Micronesia and whose photo graces the cover. My thanks to Tyler Hoobler, who has been a dependable colleague during the early stages of writing and editing. Jerry Kelly's love of literature and skill as a publisher was invaluable. And I appreciate the encouragement of colleagues and friends, many of whom appear in these pages.

CONTENTS

*"Like free winging angels,
exempt from the linear construction of time,
memory did as it pleased."*

– Oscar Hijuelos
Twain and Stanley Enter Paradise

WORDMAN

I am Wordman. It is the name I gave a character in
Eddie and the Cruisers, a film that shows up on late night
television specials like "Movies that Rock." The film,
based on my novel, stars Tom Berenger as Wordman. Set in
New Jersey, *Eddie and the Cruisers* was my second film. The
first was *Dog Day Afternoon*, starring Al Pacino. That film
was based on a *LIFE* magazine article about a bank robbery, and the subsequent hostage crisis in Brooklyn.
Dog Day Afternoon began as journalism, became a film and
then inspired a play on Broadway and in London.

Successes like these are high points in a writer's career. And
while some writers might say that they would write without
the promise of success, I would argue that writers want
readers, viewers, an audience, as well as appreciation and
respect. We don't write just for ourselves.

I am often asked how one becomes a writer. For me, it
came early and it was probably apparent to my family and
teachers before I realized it. At twelve years old, I wrote
my first travel account in the form of a diary. I'd given the
diary away shortly after I'd written it, and forgotten about
it. But on a visit to relatives in New Jersey, an aunt presented me with my handwritten account of my first sea voyage
to Europe. She'd tied together the pages with a white satin
ribbon. When I read it, I found it showed a surprising
journalistic command of detail and, for a young storyteller,
a good understanding of characters and circumstances. It
was funny. I'd clearly written it for an audience. It was an
account to be shared, and in my aunt's case, treasured.

My account ended like this: "We all said that we would not cry when we arrived in Stuttgart. Well there is where we made a mistake. We all did except for Pop, as far as I could see. Most everybody I had ever heard of was there and there were still some left over. I have never seen so much joy before and probably never will again. After that we all went to a hall where all of us could be together for a while. I got a small model ship from Tante Marta, the toy shop owner in Winnenden. It was very nice. I really like everyone. We slept at Onkel Walter's. When we were in Rotterdam, Tante Helen threw up from sea sickness even though she was no longer at sea."

It's been more than a half century since I wrote those lines. I was a kid. But there is nothing juvenile about the day-to-day account of that trip. There are scenes, characters, emotions and – as in the last sentences – a humorous, ironic talent. I was on my way to becoming a bit of a writer and a bit of a wise guy.

In recent years, I've taught writing as writer-in-residence at Kenyon College, a liberal arts college in Ohio. Some of my students have talent. Some have had considerable success, among them John Green, who wrote *The Fault in Our Stars*, *Looking for Alaska*, *An Abundance of Katherines* and other books, some of which have become films. I also taught Ransom Riggs, author of the *Miss Peregrine's Home for Peculiar Children* series and Kristen Orlando, who wrote *You Don't Know My Name*. Stephanie Danler, who wrote *Sweetbitter*, and many others who carry on Kenyon's writing tradition, have passed through my seminars and classes. This book is dedicated to those students.

One of the goals of this book is to dispel the notion that writing is easy, that you can just sit down and write. It's rarely that simple. First comes the understanding of the power of words and ideas: Reading is the breathing in. Writing is the breathing out. For readers at that first step, I have provided a list of books that I often recommend and have sometimes taught.

This book is personal. Much of it is in first person. And I have purposefully chosen to let the younger me do the talking in published articles, correspondence and other material from critics and supporters to demonstrate how my career developed. I have attempted, by example, to answer questions writers often have about how experiences and unplanned events influence and shape a career. I offer here what I have learned and taught.

In addition, I hope I can answer some of the questions writers ask: How do I get the material? How do I create the characters, the settings, the experience, the dialogue? What kind of writer am I? I began to answer these questions for myself by starting out as a journalist, a summer intern on a local newspaper when I was in college.

Like most writers I have a territory, places, people and topics that I know well. My characters, real and imagined, are drawn from my personal narrative. And I admit, I am nostalgic. I am a writer who wants to keep up with the gossip. On a recent visit, probably my twentieth, to Koror, Palau, a front-page newspaper headline read: "KLUGE VISITS AGAIN."

I am originally from New Jersey, but over the decades I've lived in Prague, Bucharest, Chicago, Los Angeles, New York City, and Honolulu. My wife, a *New York Times* foreign correspondent and later the head of the Asia Foundation in the Philippines, spent nearly seven years working in Southeast Asia. I did not waste the opportunity. From my Philippine experience, I wrote three novels and several magazine articles. Along the way, my own employment included financial writing at *The Wall Street Journal*, entertainment writing at *LIFE* magazine, freelance writing for *Playboy*, *Smithsonian Magazine*, *GEO*, *Readers Digest*, and *Rolling Stone*. All of these journalistic opportunities fed my imagination and enriched my writing.

P.F. KLUGE

JOURNALISM

JOURNALISM
The Takeoff

J ournalism. Journalist. Reporter. Today, those don't come across as compliments. When you hear them, they are often trailed by notes of annoyance, condescension: a gaggle of people competitively shouting questions at some sort of government spokesperson.

I remember better times, when a reporter was a good thing to be. Certainly, it was good for me. I started with a summer job on *The New Providence Dispatch*, where the editor could count on me when she went on vacation. After graduate school at the University of Chicago – a Ph.D. at 25 and eligible for the draft during the Vietnam War. I joined the Peace Corps, requesting an assignment to Ethiopia or Turkey: exotic cultures. But I was assigned to Micronesia, the island of Saipan, in what was then known as The United States Trust Territory of the Pacific Islands. "The Peace Corps is going to Paradise", that was the slogan. In a place I hadn't heard of, or didn't ask to go to, I was a journalist, assigned to write for and edit a magazine, *The Micronesian Reporter*.

For me, journalism was the best way to begin my career. It taught me discipline and interviewing skills and it led to other opportunities. While still a Peace Corps Volunteer, I wrote a story about a movie that was being filmed in the Rock Islands of Palau. *Hell in the Pacific* was about two men – a Japanese soldier, Toshiro Mifune, and an American soldier, Lee Marvin – who were stranded on a tiny Pacific island. I spent days on location with the crew. I found that Marvin, so often cast as a hothead, had a sensitive, thoughtful side. I wrote the article as a freelancer for *LIFE* magazine. After it appeared, Lee Marvin referred to me in a television interview as a "wet behind the ears Ph.D."

Years later, I was hired by *LIFE* magazine to cover entertainment, mostly profiles of actors at work, articles like the one about Lee Marvin. But while on a story in Los Angeles, I got a call from the New York office. It was urgent. I had to get back to New York immediately. There was a bank robbery in progress. They needed the story right away and it appeared that I was one of a very few magazine writers who was capable of producing an old-fashioned deadline-driven news story. Apparently, a couple of guys had attempted to rob a Brooklyn bank. The robbery was botched and the result was a hostage crisis. The police and hundreds of spectators were outside the bank. Television crews were filming every minute. Inside, bank employees, frightened at first, had begun to bond with the robbers, an early version of what was later called the Stockholm Syndrome.

I rushed to New York and with another reporter wrote *The Boys in the Bank*, which years later became *Dog Day Afternoon*, a Warner Brothers film.

Journalism still gets me out of the office, out of my routines and out of my comfort zone. It still forces me to figure out places and situations, to question what I see, and to interpret what it means. I tell students that there are advantages to being a stranger, which is what most journalists are. Because you're an outsider, people may tell you things they wouldn't share with their neighbors. On the other hand, there are also advantages to knowing your territory, becoming an accepted outsider with insider privileges and friends who may be interested in helping you. How do you know if you're an insider? A tip: It's when people in the places you visit talk to you about each other.

Journalism was my start and I still depend on journalism to keep me writing. But it is not the only kind of writing I do. There are novels and nonfiction, essays, articles. Journalism is the writing I do between books.

I don't teach journalism. I never did. But I believe in good journalism and promote it. At Kenyon, I was the faculty advisor to the *Collegian*, the college newspaper. And because of a generous gift from a donor, who established and endowed the P.F. Kluge Fund, I'm able to encourage responsible journalism on campus and support internships and conferences. Like many colleges, Kenyon does not have a journalism program.

When a student asks about being a writer, I often suggest journalism as a start. Though most writers will eventually find their way to the form that gives them the greatest satisfaction, I encourage students to learn the rules of writing for an audience and to embrace a fact that all journalists know; the first paragraph is the most important. Called the "lede," the first paragraphs, may be all a reader reads. Having read just a few words, or possibly a few sentences, a reader may decide to continue to read or not. While it may not be as urgent for a novelist to hook a reader immediately, the "first paragraph" test is often in evidence in bookstores.

Journalists do not have a choice, I say to my students. The lede must tell the story. "Planes tend to crash on take-off or on landing."

*"There's one map in front of me that leads from place to place
and another map in my head, going back through time,
and I have no idea where that will take me."*

Some of the places
I've written about and
sometimes called home...

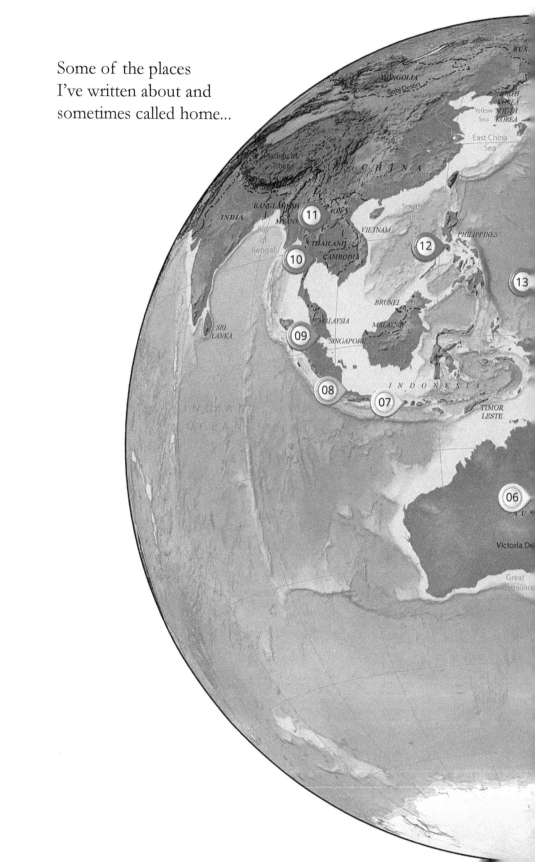

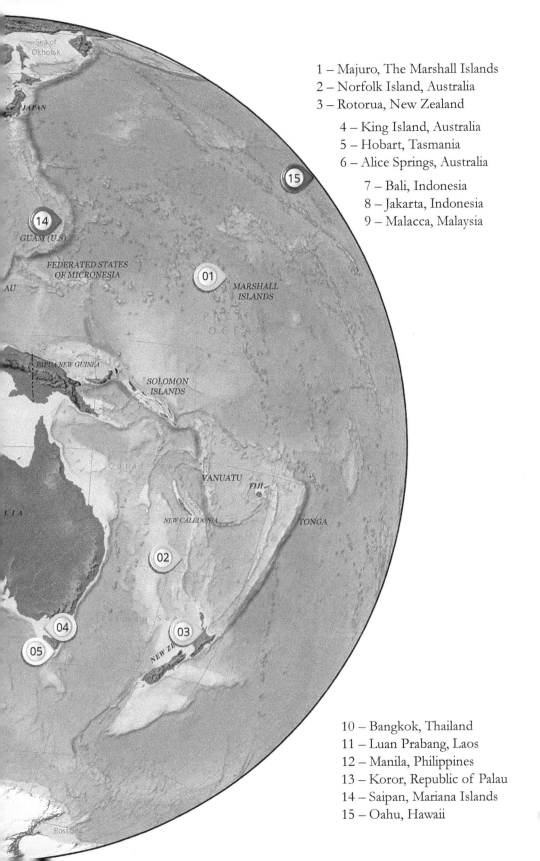

1 – Majuro, The Marshall Islands
2 – Norfolk Island, Australia
3 – Rotorua, New Zealand

4 – King Island, Australia
5 – Hobart, Tasmania
6 – Alice Springs, Australia

7 – Bali, Indonesia
8 – Jakarta, Indonesia
9 – Malacca, Malaysia

10 – Bangkok, Thailand
11 – Luan Prabang, Laos
12 – Manila, Philippines
13 – Koror, Republic of Palau
14 – Saipan, Mariana Islands
15 – Oahu, Hawaii

JOURNALISM
Travel Writing

*"I've been banging out travel columns long enough to know
when Paris would feel like Newark, and other days
when Newark could feel like Paris. That is the duplicity of the
travel-writer's dodge and the magic."*

I suspect some writers have strong reservations about travel writing, especially journalistic travel writing. Let me be the first to admit that I have sinned, repeatedly, promiscuously, profitably, globally, beyond the hope of forgiveness and repentance. *Playboy* sent me to the Philippines, as did *Rolling Stone*. *Playboy* sent me to South Africa. *Geo* dispatched me to Saipan and American Samoa. *Smithsonian* to the Palau Islands. *Islands* magazine ran my cover story on tiny Norfolk Island, midway between New Zealand and Australia. It also published a moody piece on the World War II island of Corregidor, out in Manila Bay. (I have a personal and professional weakness for islands). *National Geographic Traveler*, where I was listed as a contributing editor, sent me to Bali, Bavaria, Jerusalem, Malacca, Vienna, Tasmania, Luang Prabang, and Idaho. Those are my credentials, those are what I have to apologize for. I plead guilty.

What follows is a sample of my travel writing, first paragraphs – the take-off – giving a sense of how these stories, and adventures, begin.

Tasmania, Australia
At the End of the World

As far west from North America as I can imagine being, I stand at the edge of a pier in Hobart, Tasmania, looking out at an ocean I've been warned about. Watch those waves rolling in, I've been told, and you know they come from the Earth's depths, from realms of darkness and ice. It's in the water, in the wind, a menacing chill that says this far, and no farther. Convicts were shipped from England to this "fatal shore" in the early 1800s, and for years, the place was caricatured as static, backward, inbred. While I stand there, a van pulls up beside me. Out pops a sixtyish gent, white haired, barrel-chested, delivering cases of ginger beer to a seafood restaurant. "The next stop is Antarctica," he says, glancing at the horizon.

Malacca, Malaysia
The Spell of Old Asia

"There is no place in Malaya that has more charm," W. Somerset Maugham wrote of Malacca 81 years ago. "It has the sad and romantic air of all places that have once been of importance and live now in the recollection of a vanished grandeur."

I went to Malacca because of a Maugham story and because I loved the sound of its name. It resonated, like Zamboanga and Luang Prabang, like the lyrics of an old song. I went because the city is on the Strait of Malacca, where one-third of the world's commerce – and some 80 percent of Japan's oil – passes through a narrow channel that is one of the most heavily pirated places in the world.

I went to Malacca because I was looking for a piece of the Asia that used to be. Gridlocked, polluted, high-rise and high-priced, Asia's modern cities don't invite nostalgia. But, just a five-hour bus ride from Singapore, Malacca might still be the kind of place where Maugham sat under a fan, savoring an after-dinner brandy and a local cheroot. Or so I hoped. I'd been to Malacca for a day and a night, nearly 30 years ago: a small, sleepy, left-behind-feeling place with old colonial buildings, narrow lanes, night markets, a mix of Malays, Indians, and Chinese. The Asia of the past. Would it still be there?

The Philippines
[Guilty Pleasure #1]
Touch Me, Heal Me

Does it sound odd when I tell you that I often dream of flying halfway around the world to go to a barbershop? Like most American men, whenever my hair grows too long I go to a place in a shopping center that takes 20 minutes to cut my hair for a penny less than ten dollars. At home I shave with a disposable blade – five minutes, tops.
And something in me screams at the loss of pleasure in my life.

I lived in the Philippines, on and off, for five years. When I weigh the prospect of returning against the desire to explore new places, the part of me that thinks clearly admits that I may never get back to Manila. Yet there's a longing to return for just a few hours and for just one purpose. A guilty pleasure is a sharp, deeply imbedded memory that can pull you halfway around the world. And isn't that what travel is about? No one misses a whole country, an entire journey. We miss sensations, a taste, a time of day. A self-indulgence. A barbershop.

Luang Prabang, Laos
A Taste of Old Asia

Picture this, when you think of Luang Prabang. Picture a scene in a movie that has never been made. A woman, probably French, possibly Catherine Deneuve, no longer young but still beautiful, returns to Indochina, to the landscape of her youth, a vanished empire, a long-ago home. Across a gap of miles and years, she seeks out what she remembers, a mighty muddy river, rice fields and vegetable gardens, temples and palaces and markets, crowded streets and nameless, narrow alleys, and, most of all one of those unforgettable colonial houses...

Australia's Tasty Little Secret

An eight-seater airplane! With a propeller! When I arrive at the airport at Devonport, on the north coast of Tasmania, my heart jumps. I like small planes, short runways, and sleepy airports where they weigh your luggage and assess your body weight because all this means: small island. The small island I'm headed to, across the straits between Tasmania and Australia, is a place that I've been wondering about for years. I first heard about King Island in Sydney, or maybe it was from a foodie in Singapore. At the time, it was just excited whispers that a nowhere island produced small quantities of extraordinary cheese. If the cheeses were that exceptional, I reasoned, then King Island must be something else, an island different from the archipelagoes that build resorts and golf courses, put on a Don Ho album and wait, avidly for the world to come to their party.

Is Bali Still Paradise?

The odds are long, I admit, but I return to Bali to correct a mistake, to find what may be lost forever. In 1977, in a small gallery in the village of Ubud, I saw a painting that tempted me. Picture a Hindu temple in a forest clearing lit by a full moon. In an eerie union of the animal and the spiritual, three monkeys are perched upon a temple pillar, embracing stone gods, seeming to both blaspheme and worship at once. For whatever reason – shipping, money – I passed the painting by, a bad decision that haunts me even now. I have no idea whether the painting is great art, the product of an individual talent or a village assembly line, as common as big-eyed puppies. But I want it.

Pacific Island: Palau

This love of islands gets embarrassing. I just
phoned my travel agent and, while on hold waiting to learn whether I could get from Columbus,
Ohio, to the Pacific islands of Palau for less than
$3,000, I listened to a taped message that recount-
ed tropical island charms: swaying palms, balmy
breezes, white-sand beaches, underwater won-
derlands, Technicolor sunsets. It made me wince.
Can anyone say the word "paradise" without a
wised-up grin? We all know better, don't we? And
yet, with whole continents still unvisited, I keep
returning to a small, remote place I've seen a doz-
en times before.

For most people, Hawaii is far as they come. For
me it's a halfway point. West of Hawaii, in a huge
swath of the Pacific, there are more than 2,000
islands bound in one way or another to the United
States. From the east, they stretch from southern-
most American Samoa to the northerly Marshalls
and Marianas to Palau in the far west.

JOURNALISM
Confessions of a Travel Writer

"Most people who are travel writers are writers who travel and not travelers who decide they want to write."

L et me admit that it's strange – never fails to be strange – arriving, usually at night, to a place I may have visited often, or never. A place that everyone who lives there knows more about than I do. Infinitely more. The language, the history, the food and seasons, the politics and money, moods and humors of the place. It seems absurd – an act of arrogance, an insult to intelligence, to presume to write about an unfamiliar place. I know the complexity of foreign places. I've read Henry James. Great writers have devoted whole careers, pondering foreign countries for dozens of years and hundreds of pages, recording the lessons that travel teaches them, layer upon layer of befuddlement and enlightenment, exhilaration and disappointment, at the end concluding that, however long they stay, they will never be finished with the place or the place with them. As for me I have – at most – two weeks to report and not more than 2,500 words to report with. Can I be blamed for wondering how I got into this? Or asking myself what I think I am doing.

Most people who are travel writers are writers who travel and not travelers who decide they want to write. The ability to write is rarer, I suppose, than the desire to take

a trip that someone else pays for. Writers who travel have
an advantage. In addition to their prose style, they bring
an eye for story and for characters; they bring a sense of
place. And, most important they bring their character,
their attitude, their personae to bear, their crankiness and
humor. I am thinking of Graham Green, Aldous Huxley,
Lawrence Durrell, D.H. Lawrence and, on a slightly lower
rung, Paul Theroux, Bill Bryson and Pico Iyer. These
are not impartial, objective, documentary writers. These
are fallible narrators, nasty and nice, who make mistakes,
change their minds, test and sometime confirm their prej-
udice when they travel. They expose themselves to the risk
of foolishness and the chance of being wrong.

They will – I will – sometimes be wrong. It's inevitable.
It's desirable. Travel, it's been noted, recapitulates birth
and infancy. You come to a place where you can barely
speak; where you deal in simple phrases. Baby talk. You
eat baby food, too. Arcane ingredients, powerful spices
are withheld. Menus feature photographs for your bene-
fit, and helpful translations: "meat of pig baby, chopped
small." You take halting baby steps, under escort, to safe
places with acceptable hygiene and plumbing. Granted,
infancy is necessary for infants. It's worse for adults, mad-
dening and when I'm reminded that the word for travel
has the same root as travail – difficulty, ordeal – this is the
kind of ordeal I have in mind.

But I wouldn't want to miss it. Here's what it comes to,
the paradox of the travel writing business: that the possibilities of it are so magically high and the realities of it are
so dreadfully low. It's sad and getting sadder. With all the
world awaiting them, editors settle for hackneyed ideas,
easy targets, happy talk. Superficial reporting: conversa-

tions with waiters, taxi drivers, tourist guides. Endearing folk-wisdom from nameless locals who are too good to be true, and sometimes aren't. The editors ask for less and less: less risk, less gravity, less of the tension and disorientation that make travel an adventure. Yet writers keep coming, anxious to oblige.

Low standards. It's a matter of supply and demand. The number of travel magazines in the U.S. is finite – and shrinking. But the number of people who aspire to be travel writers – to be known as travel writers – expands. What a dream it is, to be paid to go someplace and write about it! What adventure, pleasure, prestige! There are people who will do almost anything for this. They'll pay for the trip themselves; write it off as a tax-deductible business expense, taking a $250 payment for a $2,000 trip. That's low!

And low gets lower. At the very bottom of the food chain are bottom-feeders who have turned the term "freelance" into a phrase of censure, not approval. They travel the world as predators and mendicants, their hands out, foraging for discounted or complimentary airline tickets and hotel rooms, tours and meals and gifts and favors, piecing together a livelihood, cycling and recycling their work. These people work hard, in their way. It's a rough trade. These people are knowledgeable, well-traveled, and wised up and should not be condescended to. From the vantage point of academe and scholarly conferences, they appear pathetic. Their work might be corrupt and debauched, market-driven, deeply compromised. But they deal with the world as it is: imperfect.

Now, I move to the zone of magic, high possibilities.

Travel writing is the ultimate test of one's ability to report, to come into a strange place for a short time and produce something in which truth reposes, something which will be of interest not only to an audience of distant readers but also to the people being visited, who are often curious about what a foreign writer got, and missed.

And now I offer the one thing, the one sure thing I have at the start of every story, despite all the risks and uncertainties, despite the fact that I am in a hall of mirrors. Everyone knows more about the place than I do, except one thing: *how they look to me*. And if I can make sense of that, feeling my way, sorting things out, there's hope. And the chance of something perceptive and honorable and interesting. Interesting to people who read the stories and people who appear in them. For this to happen, you have to have a story in mind, before you begin. A destination is not a story, not an idea. You need a purpose, a mission, a quest or a question. Without that, all you have is shopping, eating, touring. That's not a story. Here are some stories:

In Luang Prabang, Laos, I wondered what remained of the Royal Capitol situated in a People's Republic. Did the monarchy – which vanished in 1975, when the last king of Land of A Thousand Elephants was taken away, never to return – did the monarchy haunt the place? And did those middle-aged French tourists, rummaging around the remnants of their lost colonial Indochina find anything that resonated?

In Bali, I remembered splendid Ubud, a magical mountain town, a retreat of artists and craftsmen, surrounded by streams, terraced rice paddies. I remembered temples and markets, a slow, measured life and I wondered what was left of it. "Is Bali still Bali?" I asked. What charm might survive on this island that Nehru called "the morning of the world?"

In Tasmania – an "island at the end of the world" – I examined how a place marred by genocide of aborigines and by convict settlements had suddenly become attractive, pristine, desirable, a place of exile transformed into a safe haven, a place to escape to, not from.

King Island is a tiny spot in the Bass Straits between Tasmania and the main island of Australia. When I read that a King Island Dairy blue cheese had taken first place at an international food festival, I had a story: "the fromagerie at the end of the world."

It goes on. I rummaged around Bavaria and Austria, exploring whether small, local breweries could – and should – survive in an age of corporate consolidation and mass production. I came to Vienna, mandated to devise a perfect night in that fine city and bravely confronted a major existential question: whether to eat before or after the Staatsoper's 7 p.m. production of *The Magic Flute*. I spent two weeks in Idaho, logging 3,000 miles, moving from one hot spring to another, visiting rickety out-of-fashion resorts, new-age spas, jolting down forest trails, bathing naked in thermal springs on the edge of mountain streams, luxuriating in pine-scented air and meadows of wildflowers, searching – as the story's headline announced – for the perfect soak.

In Malacca, on the west coast of Malaysia, I visited a place that Somerset Maugham had written about. My thesis was that the retro-charms of Asia were disappearing from cutting-edge high-rise cities like Singapore and Kuala Lumpur but might yet be found in a sleepy bypassed place like Malacca. I report – and reported – that the thesis was correct. A place that the *Lonely Planet* guide advised was worth two days held me for ten.

So: you need to have an idea. And it had better be an idea that interests you. An idea for travel, not an excuse for taking a trip. It cannot stink of homework. But you have to do homework: reading, phone calls, contacts among locals, and expatriates. I worry a lot about going out on a story: ask my wife. I kill the story a dozen times in my mind, conjugate all the ways in which it's a bad idea. My worst nightmare is arriving in a place where no one will talk to me. So I prepare, I list questions, I consider answers and – like anyone who has ever gone to a new place – I rely on the kindness of strangers. And trust that someone will talk to me. That's one of the benefits of the trade. You're a travel writer. You have a reason to talk to people. And they have a reason to talk to you. And the results are often memorable. Sometimes people open up. Maybe it's because you're a writer. A foreigner. Maybe it's because they want to leave a record. Maybe it's because they hope to see you again, or know that they probably never will.

The questions you ask are not complicated or tricky. It's about where they live, what they like when they're at home, why they need to leave now and then, what they miss while they are away, what they take comfort in, what they worry about, what is their sense of the past and the future. This is the best part of travel writing: these conversations. This is what travel is about, and travel is best when I'm working, for my assignment separates me from the endless, numbing parade of tourists who enrich and stupefy the places and people they visit. In the small Pacific Islands I frequent, they have a saying about such visitors: "the same tide that carries them in carries them out." When you're writing, that changes things. You go deeper, you stay longer. You take something with you, you leave something behind. Perhaps you return.

A word on returns, on going back. I'm grateful for, even a little bit proud of the travel writing I've done, though I have lots of complaints about how editors cut and process my prose, turning my steak into hamburger. Travel writing has enriched my life and has generated some prose that makes its way into novels I've written. But the ultimate tribute is that I've sometimes returned – at my own expense – to a place I first encountered in the line of duty. And, oh, that look of shock, surprise, pleasure when people see I've come back of my own free will, that sense that they and their place were not just another item on a traveler's list of target destinations: been there, seen it, done it. That moment of return is precious to me, as a man and as a writer. That kind of connection. What was it E.M. Forster said in an epigraph to one of his novels? "Only connect".

The future of travel writing is – to the extent I see it – troubling. Lots of people want to write. Not enough care to read. Magazines dwindle and shrink. In an age of atrophied attention spans, articles get shorter. In an age of lengthening reaction times, the time it takes for an article to appear in print lengthens. One piece of mine waited four years: I almost sent birthday cards, to remind editors how long the article and its author, had been waiting.

Furthermore, the kind of narrative piece I specialize in is
endangered by a penchant for consumer-oriented service
material, gimmicky, subsidiary sidebars on handicrafts or
textiles, and lists: 10 best pasta places in Portofino, six hot
all-night dance clubs in Rio, five Bavarian castles not to
miss, et cetera, et cetera.

Editors have gotten more cautious in making assignments; they take fewer risks and gambles; their world, in
a word, has shrunk. They endorse the idea of the offbeat
but seldom stray from the beaten path. They condescend
to their readers; they hesitate to challenge. They appear
not to realize that being the fastest to follow – to follow
a market trend, a fashion, a demographic shift – is not
the same as leading. There are more and more places
they're not interested in. But if there's a Cinzano um-
brella near a beach, with three pouting svelte models
underneath, no worry. I'm glad I went where I did, when
the going was good.

There are a lot of things it pleases me to remember,
breakthroughs with people who shared insights, confidences, secrets. Even anger. I remember the journalist
I talked to in Bangkok, when I was on my way to Laos.
"The nice thing about war," he said, "is it keeps tourists
out." I remember the Pacific Islander who advised me:
"Knowledge is power. So around here people lie a lot."

I remember walking through a tropical garden with a de-
scendant of the Bounty mutineers, and I remember sitting
in a beer garden outside the world's oldest brewery, and
I remember waiting on a beach in Tasmania for mutton
birds to return from a day at sea, waiting in fading light
while they landed, and walked to the burrows they'd made

in the sand, where their offspring were hungry and then, from below the ground I heard the gurgling, chirping sound of an evening meal.

One last moment, I toured the Old Royal Palace in Luang Prabang, a mix of regal furniture, gilded walls, red paint, dark wood and, well, junk. Souvenirs. Some pebbles from the moon. Pictures of Lyndon Johnson. Keys to the city of, as I recall, Birmingham, Alabama. A victrola with dusty vinyl records. All sad. Outside, I noticed a non-descript metal building, a warehouse, maybe. It turned out to be the royal garage. A small payment followed. I slipped open the door. There sat an Edsel! One of Detroit's worst failures, a total flop; now of course a collector's item. Vanished car, vanished monarchy. I felt lucky, I got luckier. I was alone, unsupervised. I reached for the door handle. Amazingly, it opened. I slid behind the wheel, startled at what I was getting away with. I looked at the dashboard, at the odometer that recorded at just what mileage the Kingdom of Laos had run out of gas.

I realize that there are many complaints, protests, reservations about travel writing: that it embodies and encodes stereotypes and clichés, that it commodifies and marginalizes. Maybe so. Sometimes. But people will travel, in this fallen world, they will not stay home. And the vision of politically correct, invincible, forbearing, invariably decorous traveler is a dream – and not a very happy dream at that. People will travel. In colonial, post-colonial, neo-colonial or global times they will travel; they will travel to and from developed, developing, undeveloped and imploding nations. As long as this is so, there will be, or should be, a place for travel writing. Possibly a place of honor.

JOURNALISM
Readers Respond

"I write in order to be read, to connect, to inspire, to entertain. It pleases me when I do. And it especially pleases me when readers let me know that they took the journey with me."

Hawaii…5 a.m. was published in *National Geographic Traveler*.

Hawaii…5 a.m.

If you dream of islands, dream of how they are at dawn, on the border between night and day, sleep and waking. Dream of them when they are cool and hushed, before heat and light chase the dream away. I learned this lesson – you could say it dawned on me – years ago. It's been confirmed many times since, across the Pacific and around the world.

It's still dark in Honolulu as I head on a highway that takes me to the eastern side of Oahu, past black basalt boulders and blowholes, waves geysering into the air. I stop at Sandy Beach, where locals greet the new day, some of them blowing conch shells to welcome morning. I continue to Waimanalo, where I find a beach, shaded by casuarina trees, that goes on for miles. Then I drive uphill on the Pali Highway and turn onto Old Pali Road, which runs through a rain forest, a tunnel with eucalyptus trees meeting overhead, moss, vines, blossoms. It is cool and green and quiet. A perfect morning in paradise.

A blog by Sahar responds to Hawaii:

A couple of years ago I read an article in *National Geographic Traveler* by P.F. Kluge. The piece was part of the magazine's best 24-hours on earth cover story, which begins in Hawaii with Kluge. In his opening sentence, he writes, "if you dream of islands, dream of how they are at dawn on the border between night and day, sleep and waking." I've never really thought about visiting Hawaii, but after reading this one line, Hawaii meant something more to me. I was connected to the place inexplicably.

How is it that writers like Kluge make an impact on us? What is it about their words that make us contemplate booking a plane ticket, packing a suitcase? Inspiring us to make our way to some part of the world we've never thought of visiting before? Why does travel writing get under our skin in this way?

These days, I'm much more mindful of sunrise wherever I might be in the world. Perhaps, one day, I'll be lucky enough to visit Oahu and bear witness to the spectacle Kluge speaks of, but either way, my life is richer for having read *5 a.m. Hawaii*. It is the only article I've ever pinned to the corkboard in my home. More than a story, Kluge's words are an affirmation: *"Dawn is when you plan your day, your future, sunset is when you contemplate your past."* For travel junkies and writers aspiring to greatness like me, Kluge is the real rockstar.

I also write to encourage exploration and discovery. And I've found that readers often understand, as I do, that travel is more than going places.

The Ocean
National Geographic Traveler

On a ferry from Manhattan to Staten Island, on a voyage across the Drake Passage to Antarctica, on a copra-collecting ship nosing among tiny Pacific atolls, on a floating university circling the globe, it never fails. I stand at the railing, even though there's no land in sight; I stand there at night when there's nothing but stars, and I sense that there's something about oceans that I need, that everybody needs, something that a life spent wholly on land and inland would be missing. It has nothing to do with sunny, sandy beaches, diving, fishing, or purchasing coastal real estate.

The ocean puts you on the edge of infinity and eternity. It covers almost three-fourths of the earth; it could drown Mount Everest; it generates perfect storms and total calms. It puts you in touch with the way things are and were, for even at this late date, every ocean voyage offers an excitement that's both ancient and childlike.

Standing at that railing, studying the horizon, something in you wants to shout "Land Ho!" Like Columbus encountering America, Cook probing for a great southern continent, Magellan circling the globe, you feel some old and potent magic. And like them, you hope to discover a new world.

From: Valerie N.
Norristown, PA

Dear Mr. Kluge,

I simply must write and tell you how moved I felt upon reading your description of *The Ocean* in "National Geographic Traveler." I have already quoted you in discussions ("*...The ocean puts you on the edge of infinity and eternity...*" – it sounds as poetic as Shakespeare) and sent a snippet of your quote to a special gentleman in The Netherlands who lived a great deal of his life at sea as an engineer with Holland America Line.

You have so beautifully captured the wonder I feel when land slips away and I am confronted with a universe of stars that are normally obscured by the pollutants of population and overcrowding. You really stated what is always in my heart – the thrill of being afloat on what seems the uncomplicated, unchangeable, uncolonized part of the globe. And always it inspires me to see beyond myself and the smallness of my own life, and to think across boundaries and cultures and dogma.

For me, the best part of a sea voyage is to climb up to the top near the stack late at night, while everyone else is doing their midnight buffet. I feast on the sky and the sounds of a ship parting the waters. It's magic.

Well, didn't mean to be so long-winded. I just want to thank you for writing such a beautiful piece. I will frame it and keep it forever.

A WRITER'S LIFE

A WRITER'S LIFE
The Chances You Take

*"You have an idea, an experience. Maybe you have a character,
a place. Perhaps you have a single phrase, or the lyrics of a song.
Whatever the trigger and regardless of how the plot develops,
the writing is just the beginning."*

S o you're a writer," someone will say to me. I can hear admiration, even envy in their words. It's as if I have managed to become what many other people want to be. There's much more that I could add, though: dealing with agents and editors, waiting for reviews, hoping for recognition…and heavy sales. Good things happen, sometimes. But there's no guarantee.

Writing, freelance writing in particular, is not a lucrative career choice for most. The Author's Guild, a professional organization, keeps track of what book writers make. Full time writers, as a group, seldom make more than $25,000. That figure hasn't budged for decades.

For most writers, royalties and advances are not enough to pay the expenses of writing a book, especially one that needs research, travel, interviews. And the opportunity for contracts and assignments are fewer now that magazines, newspapers and numerous print publications have dried up. Self-publishing, e-books and other delivery options have eroded the relationships between agents, publishers and writers. In short, it's tough being a writer.

As this book chronicles, I've taken advantage of opportunities and I've occasionally gotten lucky. I've turned down some offers. For example, I don't do "as told to books" or edit other writers. For fifteen years I was a full-time writer, trusting that being unemployed, except for freelance work and work on my own books, was a smart thing to do. To dedicate yourself exclusively to writing is a gamble. For me, it was worth it.

A WRITER'S LIFE
Life after *LIFE*

Note to readers: Rather than looking back and recreating a time, a mood, a circumstance, I've let the prose created by my younger self speak for me. When I left daily journalism I had to trust my ability to survive as a writer.

Life after *LIFE* leads to *Dog Day Afternoon*
Kenyon Alumni Bulletin
Published 1983

Whenever I am back in New York, around 50th Street, I get the sort of emotional tug you often feel when you return to a place where you used to be happy. I glance up at the Time-Life Building, up 30 floors or so, to where my office used to be. I liked it, up there. Coffee and conspiracy were in the air, jobs and bylines and a sense that accomplishments were measurable in time and money. I liked the compartmentalization of time, leaving home to go to work, returning home at night, just like my father, except I carried a briefcase and the old man took along a black lunch pail. Also, there were late nights with beer and sandwiches while waiting for the magazine to close; books and albums that came in for review; whole lockers full of stationery and pencils. *LIFE* magazine: I miss it sometimes. It was my last regular grown-up job. When the weekly *LIFE* magazine died, I sensed that my life would be changed utterly, and it was. Up there on the 30th floor, I was an employed journalist. Down here, I think of myself as a writer. And I live, sometimes happily, in the land of accidents.

My first accident was *Dog Day Afternoon*. It was an accident that a mass market magazine like *LIFE* should dispatch another reporter and myself to piece together an account of a bizarre bank robbery-hostage situation perpetrated in Brooklyn. It was an accident that the magazine published the piece, that a talent agent who wanted to be a movie producer read it on a plane, that he persuaded his client, Al Pacino, to portray a gay bank robber, and that the film prospered so robustly that not even the most polished West Coast accountants could deny me the substantial share of profits to which my less than 3,000 magazine words entitled me.

Now there are some interesting lessons in all this. Number one is that it is nice to shake checks out of envelopes. The proceeds from *Dog Day Afternoon* have sustained me through years of novel-writing, travel and plain brooding. Number two is that, beyond writing the original piece, my role in the process that rewarded me was passive and fortuitous. I'm the boss when the pages are blank: after that, things change. And that brings me to the central paradox of the writer's trade, these days. You're probably not going to make a living out of your life's work, not directly out of it, not out of what editors and publishers pay you. You need something else. You need for accidents to happen. But accidents, by definition, are untimed and uncontrolled. For years, I've been telling friends that the concatenation

of events which resulted in *Dog Day Afternoon* was
wholly unrepeatable. You can't count on anything
like that happening twice, I say. Then again, there
is a film based on my second novel, *Eddie and the
Cruisers*. So who knows? Maybe, just once, lightning
strikes twice.

I've attempted to make a tenuous positive out of
two distinct negatives. The first negative is magazine writing. I have four cabinets full of magazine articles I have written for hire. I don't bother
clipping the articles any more: scrapbooks have
gone the way of yearbooks and I concede the truth
of a line I read somewhere which said that "In life
there is no senior year." So there they sit, a couple
hundred pounds of confetti, of in-and-out quickly,
of curiosity worked up for the occasions. *GEOs*,
Smithsonians, *New Wests*, and the tidy packet of *TV
Guide* pieces that I call my "little magazine period."
What can I say of such a miscellany? The eruption
of Mt. St. Helens. Survivalists in Utah. Basket-
ball scandals. Solar-powered airplanes. The prime
minister of Western Samoa. The sheriff of Truth
or Consequences, New Mexico. The pilot who
dropped the big one on Hiroshima. John Wayne.
Flip Wilson. Japanese bonehunters on Saipan.

Magazine articles are a mixed bag, and I don't mean
simply that the subjects are varied, or the styles, or
the lengths. I mean that I hate having them and I
hate not having them. They disrupt my schedule,
usher me and my notebook into the presence of a
great many people whom the Kenyon of my time
would have known as "screamers."

The work is hard, the results are perishable, and the pay is a little better than the Peace Corps. On the other hand, it gets me out of the house, keeps me in print, and greatly impresses friends and relatives who can't manage to find, or buy, my books.

At worst, magazine writing can make you feel like a literary Fuller Brush man, ringing doorbells, taking orders, kicking dogs. But there are triumphs. The odds against doing good works in a magazine are high. You're up against editors, many of whom have approximately the same idea at the same time. You're up against other writers, sweaty-palmed journalism school graduates who are willing to give the story more work than it's worth and might, by accident, make you look bad. You're also up against the subjects themselves, and here you confront that widening moat of litigation, flackery, manipulations and distrust which separates writers from truth (or truth from writers). Sometimes I think it's precisely because the circumstances of reporting are so ludicrous, the situation so artificial, that I find the work challenging.

Win, lose or draw, magazine work is perishable. Books may not be immortal, but anyway they last a little longer. I belong to a generation that believed books – novels – are the writing that mattered. Books put you on the scoreboard; everything else was batting practice. I read about three books for every movie I see. And the time I spend on books is the most important time. My first novel, drawing on years in Micronesia, was *The Day That I Die*, published, sort of, by Bobbs-Merrill in 1976. A

youthful book, it had Japanese stragglers, shifty
politicians, wandering journalists, Jacobean plot-
ting. It had some writing-from-the heart about
places I love and it had oversimplified female
characters I blame entirely on four years at an all-
male college in the sticks. My second novel, *Eddie
and the Cruisers* (Viking Press, 1980) had New Jersey,
rock and roll, and melancholy, plus what I hope
turns out to be the definitive account of a pre-co-
educational Kenyon dance weekend. Number three
concerns the American suppressions of the Philippines insurrection in 1900. Now these books, and
a couple of others I'm not talking about, are what
matter to me. They test, display, contain whatever
talents I have. But get this straight: I'll be damned
if I can write fiction all the time. After a couple
months, invention flags, plot tangles, characters
stare back to you and even sentence cadence falls
apart. Writing fiction in today's market begins to
feel like you've climbed out on the end of the lon-
gest possible branch on the rottenest possible tree.
That's when you start wanting magazines to call.
Or better yet, movies.

I wonder what my neighbors think of me. Most
mornings, they know I walk my dog, smoke a
cigar and work the crossword. Afternoons, I run
a lot and I get kidded for taking afternoon siestas.
Nights are a mystery, but I am known to play slow-
pitch softball on weekends and I have a certified
attachment to *Family Feud*. I disappear for weeks
at a time. I'm writing this, for instance, in Manila,
with last night's San Miguels trickling down my
arms. I guess my neighbors would say I don't have

a grown up job. I guess they're right. I'm a writer.
I'm doing the best I can. And *that*, as Damon Run-
yon remarks, is a greatly overcrowded occupation
along Broadway.

A WRITER'S LIFE
A Perfect Place to Write

Writers often dream of the perfect place to write: a house in Malibu, a cottage on the coast of Maine, a snug hideout in Paris. The reality is that most writers are working at the kitchen table or at a small desk in a guest bedroom or in the basement. You'll take any room that has a door that closes and leaves you alone in the quiet.

I have an office now, a space separate from the house. But I remember trying to get the right circumstances in small apartments or hotel rooms when I had some time to work. I once used an apartment of friends in Mammoth Lakes, CA. It was off season for vacationers and skiers. The place was deserted, a scene out of *The Shining*. It was lonely. Complete isolation was not the perfect condition for me. So, like many writers, I decided to go to a writers' colony. In fact, I went to the MacDowell Colony twice.

One Month on the Word Farm
Los Angeles Times, 1979

Writers and would-be writers are notorious for carrying on about the ideal place to work: a garret, a gate house, a cabin in the woods. With a quiet place, plain food, no distractions, we could all bring home the big one.

For 70 years, the MacDowell Colony, a 400-acre retreat in Peterborough, N.H. has been quietly calling our bluff. It provides exactly what we've always claimed we needed to do our best work: peace and quiet, bed and board, for as little as a week or as long as three months. The charge: as much or as little as you can afford to pay.

Some 200 writers, artists, musicians, photographers, film-makers, chosen by peer committees from four or five times as many applicants, find their way to the MacDowell Colony each year. Some are famous. Thornton Wilder, one hears at least daily, wrote "Our Town" while at MacDowell. Aaron Copland, James Baldwin, Leonard Bernstein, Studs Terkel all passed through. So have hundreds of obscurities. And that, for a newly arriving colonist, can be something of a comfort.

My turn at MacDowell came last month. With one novel published, another circulating and a third half-written, I paid the taxi driver who'd driven me through maple syrup country from Keene and feeling like a beanie-wearing freshman all over again, stepped into Colony Hall to register. I remember thinking how shrewd I'd been to ask for less than a month, when I could have requested two or three times as long. I could stand anything for a month. And I complimented myself for scheduling my stay at MacDowell to coincide with the last weeks of road-work for the New York Marathon. That way, even if I didn't write a scratch, I could write it all off as training. Did I write the big one? No, but I ran it…

Half an hour after arriving, I'd registered and settled in. I was a "colonist." Then, as now, the term
seemed inappropriate. It suggested that I should
be out repairing stone walls, tapping maples, bail-
ing hay. Instead, I was nesting in one of the more
than 30 studios that dot the MacDowell estate. My
clothes were in my dresser, my manuscript spread
out on the table, and there were five full hours to go
before the supper bell would ring out across the pas-
tures. I had just begun to learn what occurs to every
newcomer at MacDowell: the days are enormously
long, three times as long as anyplace else. Morning,
afternoon and night loom like separate 24-hour en-
tities. It's as if you had three chances to accomplish
your day's work. Work mornings and you were doing
well. Work mornings and afternoon, you were really
cooking. Work morning, noon and night and…well,
that never happened to me.

Another lesson from that first day, nobody was
watching me. Nobody but me was keeping track
of my work. How could they? One of the colony's two rules is that no one – artist, administrator,
lover – drops in on a colonist's studio uninvited.
(The other rule prohibits smoking in the woods.) I
quickly realized that I could spend a full month at
MacDowell sleeping. Or working crosswords. Or
just sitting in my room watching maples turn and
shed. But nobody can do that for a month. So I
decided I might as well write.

That first night, before supper, I studied the names on the mailboxes in Colony Hall. Alfred A. Knopf wasn't among them. Scratch one fantasy. Or Lola Falana. Scratch another. In fact there were no names I recognized, no big reputations to contend with. Then the dining hall started filling up. The 20 unfamiliar names became people. And, in the month ahead, the people became indelible.

There was the 84-year-old Yankee poet who infuriated me by referring, despite my patient correction, to Dodger second-baseman "Lopez." The short-story writing woman who pronounced "poetry" as "poi-tree," as if you might plant a grove of them in Hawaii. The Pulitzer-winning biographer and sardonic composer I duelled at horseshoes. The female sculptor, a veteran on the colony circuit, who told of MacDowell's two closest counterparts, stately Yaddo near Saratoga, N.Y., and near-tropical Ossebaw Island, off the coast of Georgia. The writing social worker who tipped me to clandestine cockflights in the Bronx. The white-haired poet whose excruciating, carefully wrought poems on the ending of a marriage I always thought of as the "breaking-up-is-hard-to-do cantos." The painter who nervously brushed his teeth before starting his self-portrait. Before long they were all characters, all vivid and dear. And I became a character myself. Mr. Six-Pages-a-Day. The fool who ran to Willa Cather's grave in Jaffrey Center, 18 miles round trip.

The MacDowell Colony isn't a symposium or a colloquium. There's no formal program, no organized socializing and this meant that meals became events of extraordinary importance. The dining hall was the arena, the promenade, the crucible. Breakfasts were liveliest: three cups of coffee, endless talking. Evening meals were different. Conversation came harder then: the day's work depleted our supply of sentences. This was the time for pool, horseshoes, savage Ping-Pong. But the meal that most characterizes MacDowell is lunch.

Usually, I started thinking about lunch around 10. Sometimes, if work was sluggish, I'd take a nap. I never felt guilty about these morning naps. "Topping off the tank," I called it. There was always more time. Time was the essence of the place. Around noon the lunch truck crunched down the driveway, my picnic hamper and a dozen others in the back. The driver stopped, quietly deposited the hamper on the doorstep, and drove off.

I liked that. No matter that I was waiting. No matter that I would have loved an interruption. The assumption was that I was William Coleridge, smack in the middle of "Kubla Khan." So quiet please. And thank you.

Not everyone prospers at MacDowell. There are tales and jokes of freakouts, disappearances, pick-ups and deliveries from the funny farm, manic-depressive wanderings through the woods. But for every early departure there are dozens of colonists who seek an extension of their stay. To my surprise, I was one of them. The work was going well, but that's not what made me stay. The place itself had captured me. I liked the idea that the woods were full of people as worried and exhilarated as I was. That's what made it hard to leave. Solitary labor: We were all in it together.

I saved the best for last. The last morning, I took down the "tombstones": wooden boards that hung on my studio wall. Everyone who'd come to the studio before me had written his name, his trade, his date of residence. There were names I recognized: a Pulitzer winner. A Broadway playwright. A Vietnam novelist. And a lot of names I didn't know. I wrote my name on the tombstone and returned it to the wall. My successors would take pleasure knowing, or not knowing, who I was. The colony experience was over.

THE BUSINESS
OF WRITING

THE BUSINESS OF WRITING
How I Write

"A writer is alone at the start, when the pages are blank."

Isometimes wonder how many books are begun and never finished, how much ambition and talent falls short. With more than a dozen books, let me offer some practical advice. No guarantees. But what has worked for me, might work for you.

1. I work alone. No one else is in the room. No music. I save that for when I am typing. Yes, typing. I share my office with five typewriters, one of which is 100 years old.

2. The first draft is handwritten. I cannot imagine typing, let alone composing, on a computer. This will surely separate me from a majority of my contemporaries, but it connects me with scores of great writers who mean a lot to me.

3. I never ask anyone to read opening pages. Enthusiasm is suspect at this stage and criticism can end a friendship.

4. I arrive at my office after breakfast, a third cup of coffee and *The New York Times*. When the crossword puzzle is finished, I'm still holding a pen. I had better do something with it.

5. I can't, I'm not sure anybody can, plan a novel from beginning to end. Granted, you have intentions, possibilities,

decisions to make. Some things you can count on such as a place and a cast of characters. You have intentions, plans which may sustain you or be abandoned.

6. A novel is a mix of memory, lived experience and imagination. Fictitious? Yes, of course. The story isn't true. But it has truth in it, one hopes.

7. Five pages a day. That feels right. If you write in what might be a creative frenzy, you're exhausted. I prefer breaking at the bottom of the page – it could be in the middle of a paragraph – knowing that the other half paragraph will be there when I return.

8. It pleases me to see the pile of pages grow. I'm writing. Editing can wait. But every thirty pages or so I review what I have for the sake, I tell myself, of continuity. Who am I kidding? I'm hoping that what I read is okay. Better than okay.

9. When I'm closing in on the ending, I look back through the manuscript. It's not reading. It's not orderly. I grab a handful of the manuscript to make sure it feels like an accomplishment, complete, tangible.

10. So there it is… my book. At this stage, I'm the only reader. And I feel a sadness because I will miss this creative time. Now it will go to my agent, who'll send it out to editors. It might be sent to several editors, hoping that enough of them will like it that there's a bidding war to acquire it. A bidding war! But, that might not happen. If not, my agent will send the book to one publisher after another until there's an offer, or it doesn't find a home. Rejection. It happens to every writer.

11. I've published 13 books. They've all had editors. But, I've never had to work for more than 15 minutes on any change they've suggested. Usually it's something small, inconsequential, a fix in the manuscript's first pages. So there! They can say they edited! My apologies to the editors who strive to do a good job, but my advice to writers is, find someone who is not a friend to read it.

THE BUSINESS OF WRITING
My Team

Hammond, Underwood, Royal, Corona. These are members of my team – old typewriters. One is a century old. A couple of them are rare. They are all heavy black machines with hard-to-find ribbons and increasingly hard-to-find repairmen. But, they don't crash. They don't need a power source or updating. They are reliable.

My writing process is likely to seem quaint, primitive, retarded. But it works for me. I don't compose on my typewriters. My first drafts are handwritten, often in lined notebooks that I buy at discount stores. I don't buy the sedate nicely-bound ones. I prefer the ones with super heroes or dogs on the cover. None cost more than a couple of dollars. As I write, I measure my progress in used pencils and stacked notebooks.

I am not a writer who depends on inspiration. I'm not a romantic. I fall back on decades of reading and writing to guide the shape and the rhythm of a book. I don't begin to write until after I've worked out the plot and characters. It sometimes takes weeks, even months, to think it through. But once I begin to write, I start at the beginning and write through to the end. I don't edit as I go. I often reread what I wrote the day before, but I don't review much more than that. And I don't depend on inspiration or a burst of creativity that might grip me and encourage a writing marathon. I write about five pages a day, stopping at the bottom of the last page, perhaps in mid-sentence, so that I can begin again, completing that sentence and moving on the next day.

I work in silence. I am focused. I don't have reference material or notes or anything to distract me. When the manuscript is complete, I will double-check facts and spelling. But I am a clean writer. And, I am a brutal editor of my own work. Once I am satisfied, I turn my typed manuscript over to a typist, who puts it on a thumb drive and prints out a copy for me.

I don't object to writing on a computer. But the typewriters that are displayed on a long bench in my office are the tools of my trade. They connect me to the writers I admire. Good company.

THE BUSINESS OF WRITING
Agents

In black-and-white films of the previous century, an agent is often portrayed as a savvy dealmaker with standing reservations at the best restaurants and access to publishing kingmakers. He – it's seldom a woman – has a reputation and impressive victories in the cut-throat competition for talent. Agents in these films are about deals and power and money.

The reality, then and now, is that agents do make connections and deals. And, they are often essential to a writer's success. They provide valuable introductions and work out strategies that are crucial to your career. In fact, it is nearly impossible to be well-published without the negotiating talent of a good agent. Reading contracts is not how I want to spend my time. My agent is my dealmaker. And like a good agent, he is also a coach, confidant and critic.

I've had a few agents over the decades. My first was suggested by a friend. It helped that I was living in New York City when I finished my first book and that I lived in a building where other artists and writers lived. My agent helped me sell my early fiction and she helped educate me about publishing. She became a good friend, someone I trusted.

It is important to trust your agent. I am confident that my current agents are as capable of handling negotiations for films and theater deals as they are at managing my negotiations for the sale of my fiction and nonfiction. My agent is my business partner and my adviser. He often has my Power of Attorney to act on my behalf. He has talked me out of bad decisions and steered me in thoughtful ways.

Not all agents have the same strengths. Some are very good at contracts. Others are very good at nurturing young talent. Still others have extraordinary contacts based on a track record of successful sales. Granted, any author can concoct a list of desirable publishers. But a good agent knows editors who might respond favorably to your book's setting, location or characters. And, your agent may be crucial to navigating the publishing world, which now has multiple ways to approach the market including digital books, downloaded audio and other ways of delivering information and entertainment.

Because your success is your agent's success, a healthy partnership is crucial. Unlike a lawyer, your agent doesn't charge by the hour. Agents get paid when you get paid. So, you both take a risk on your talent.

THE BUSINESS OF WRITING
Publishers

Years ago I discovered the work of Maxwell Perkins, who discovered Ernest Hemingway, F. Scott Fitzgerald, Marjorie Kennan Rawlings and Thomas Wolfe. Perkins acquired, shaped, defended their books. An editor of genius, and a genius editor.

Famous writers, famous editors, famous publishing houses – the combination is magic. And it happened at Random House, which was established in 1927. Like many other writers, I wanted to be published by Random House, where William Faulkner, Sinclair Lewis, Robert Penn Warren and scores of literary giants found a home. When my first nonfiction book, *The Edge of Paradise*, was accepted and published by Random House, I felt "well published."

Publishing has changed a great deal in recent years. Boutique publishing companies offer a limited list of books each year. University presses have become more influential. And like other industries, consolidation has created mega-publishers. In 1998 Bertelsmann, the German media giant, bought Random House, which became a large complicated company having acquired, merged or absorbed a half-dozen other publishers including Penguin, Doubleday, Knopf and Crown, all of which were managed from the Penguin Random House Tower in Manhattan.

Your agent's task is to find the right publisher for your book, one that employs just the right editor to make the most of your efforts. And, if you are lucky enough to have a book that interests several publishers, you and your agent hope for a bidding war, or possibly a "two-book" deal with enough of an "advance" to help support you for at least a year. But it is more likely that you'll have a one-book deal. And, there may be years between the book you sold and the next one. And even if you had a reasonable success with the previous book, you may find that you will still go through a submission process for your next book as if it is your first, not your second or tenth.

I've often thought that it would be wonderful to write a book that just sails through the process from idea to book to editing to printing to reviews to bookstores/distribution to critical acclaim to movie/play to surprising success. That's a lot to ask. But to be honest, I would be happy just to be "well published."

Like most writers, I've had many publishers. While Random House published *The Edge of Paradise* in hardcover, it remains in print in paperback, published by the University of Hawaii Press. Overlook Press printed or reprinted four of my novels – *Master Blaster*, *A Call from Jersey*, *Gone Tomorrow* and *Eddie and the Cruisers*. Overlook is now out of business. Some of my work has been printed internationally. My nonfiction book, *Alma Mater: A College Homecoming*, which was originally published by Addison-Wesley, was republished by the University of Beijing Press.

Like every writer, I want to see my books in print forever. I want to see the print-on-demand numbers soar. I want to see lots of orders on Amazon, which has changed how books are marketed and sold. It does sadden me to see many bookstores flounder and die, but I am happy to see independent bookstores and independent publishers claim their place.

THE BUSINESS OF WRITING
Independent Publishing

Jerry Kelly published *Keepers*, my collection of essays. During the process I began to understand how complicated publishing is and how dedicated, committed and talented a small publisher must be. I asked him what, besides a love of literature, led him into publishing. This was his response:

Small press, a personal wellspring

Independent publishing intrigued me as a young college student, years ago. I was fascinated that Walt Whitman had self-published his very first 1855 edition of *Leaves of Grass* as a pocket-sized booklet cradling 12 untitled poems. Working with friends who owned a small print shop in Brooklyn, he hand-set the type for much of the book himself, and hand-sold it wherever he saw an opportunity. He left the title and his name off the cover, using only a small engraving of himself as a frontispiece. And, on the back cover, he daringly quoted a letter he'd gotten from Ralph Waldo Emerson praising his poems — the first known use of a cover blurb. Emerson was reportedly miffed that Whitman had done so without his permission.

In conversations with poet Robert Creeley, with whom I studied in the 1970s, we had much discussion of small presses. Bob had run his Divers Press from Mallorca in the 1950s, publishing modest editions of poets Charles Olson, Robert Duncan, and Paul Blackburn, among others, and had overseen the printing of the literary journal

Origin and *The Black Mountain Review* there as well. I once
climbed a sea wall in Palma de Mallorca to drop into what
remained of the original Mossén Alcover print shop Bob
had used to print and bind that work (… "just amazingly
accommodating, there and then…") — he told me exactly where it was located and how to get there. The shop, its
roof long since blown out to sea, had been laid to waste
by decades of wind and crashing waves, with only rubble
remaining — for certain, no neat stacks of Divers Press
books or *The Black Mountain Review* (a faint hope I'd nur-
tured). But it was still a thrill to find that place, to reflect
on the work completed there – a wellspring for those later
known as the Black Mountain Poets.

Small press publishing has its roots in the international
Arts and Crafts Movement, which flourished in Europe
and North America from 1880 to 1920. The movement
was a response to "a perceived decline in standards…
associated with machinery and factory production," and
dismissed contemporary art and design as "excessively
ornate, artificial, and ignorant of the qualities of the
materials used."

In contemporary terms, small presses are a growing
response to dominant global corporate publishing. More
personal, less profit-driven, smaller independent publishers tend to work closely with one author at a time,
producing editions for which the author has strong
input not only in the text but often, too, in the design,
packaging, and presentation to an audience. Poet Robert
Duncan chose to publish his work "with persons, rather
than houses" and, for many emerging and marginal writers, making connection with a small press can represent
the best way to get their work into print. Established

writers have used small press to publish work in which a larger publisher had no interest, or regarded as un-marketable. Late in life, Kurt Vonnegut chose to publish with indie presses to support their cause, his name and work having wide currency by then. It was a cool boost to those devoted to the small trade.

Now, with digital book-design tools and on-demand printing, many persons have become indie publishers of their own work, or of others' books. For my part, I was most keen on the process of making books in the company of other authors, bringing work to light that might otherwise remain private while also sharing in the frisson of creation. Working for tech companies in the 1970s and 1980s, I had my hands on exciting new digital tools, and began making small saddle-stitched booklets of friends' work. My first perfect-bound book was a collection of poems by Ralph Fletcher, a pal from high school, who was then teaching teachers how to engage students in poetry activities in the classroom. *Water Planet* was a small hit and Ralph became nationally known for his educational consulting work, as well as for his subsequent books with larger publishers.

As I developed skills with typography, book design, and print production, I was able to work with poets, novelists, and writers whose work I admired.

Fielding Dawson was one such — having studied at Black Mountain College in the 1950s and written in lower Manhattan for years, Fielding was very keen on having a hand in every detail of his books' production. Working together in his loft on 19th Street, near Union Square, we sweated all the details for a collection entitled

The Land of Milk & Honey, published by my XOXOX
Press in 2001. Prior to that, we'd worked together on a
collection of letters between a woman in Cooperstown,
New York and her lifelong best friend; they had married
two brothers, and their correspondence formed a lively
portrait of mid-century small-town American life. It
was for that book that Fielding came up with the imprint name — "how about XOXOX? — like, you know,
people put at the end of a letter or postcard — hugs
and kisses!" We used that imprint name for Grace Kull's
book of letters, *Dear Bert,* in 2000, and I continued to
use it thereafter. Fielding passed away in 2002 as we
were working on his next story collection, *The Dirty Blue
Car.* His partner Susan Maldovan and I saw that project
through to publication in 2004.

Sadly, in my two years of study at Kenyon, I never
took a class given by Perry Lentz or PF Kluge. But
working alongside them on their books (Perry's *Perish
From the Earth* and PF's *Final Exam, Keepers* and *Wordman*) was a literary engineering master class. I'll always
be grateful for those opportunities.

At Kenyon College, it's been a particular delight to
complete publishing projects with Perry, PF, Loranne
Temple, Paul Strauss, Susan Rothenberg, Peter Rutkoff,
Charlene Fix, Fred Andrle, Steve Schaefer, Harry Mar-
ten, Michael Barich, Bruce Haywood, Patrick Meanor,
Galbraith Crump, Robert Hamburger, Jordi Alonso, Gus
Franza, Mike Newell, and Bishop Bill Swing, among
others. I've had help from alert proofreaders and insightful editors like my good friend Kaitlin Tebeau, a
2012 Kenyon grad.

When people ask how the press has done, I tell them it's not made me rich, nor poor. In any arts enterprise, break-even is a good place to be if you fail to catch lightning in a bottle.

Bottom line, the work itself is enriching. Having an intimate relationship with a manuscript and taking it to the point where type is aligning on pages has always been a specific delight for me. Laboring in a deep quiet night with others' words, seeing pages form up well and projects move toward completion brings great satisfaction and comfort — exceeded only by the thrill of handing an author the first copy of their book. That experience, multiplied though the years, has been the real payoff.

I'm grateful to every writer I've published for the honor of handling their work, and for all the rich learning shared along the way.

THE BUSINESS OF WRITING
Praise

When the book is finished your work is not done. Your agent, and surely your publisher, will ask who likes your book besides you. Sure, your publisher will make an effort to circulate the book. Your agent may even have a short list of possible readers willing to provide a glowing assessment of your work that's worthy of a cover endorsement. But it will be largely up to you. How many friends have you got?

Luckily writers do try to help one another. A former student, Ransom Riggs, the author of the *Miss Peregrine's Home for Peculiar Children* series that director Tim Burton turned into a wildly successful film, was extremely generous with his praise: "I read your manuscript on two long flights (to and from London) and it was the ideal travel companion," he said in an email about *The Williamson Turn*. "I genuinely enjoyed it – the next best thing to actually sailing around the world myself...Written with a seasoned traveler's eye for detail, it's a sharp, thoughtful take on what it means to confront the world as an American, and a surprising, wistful tale of second comings and second chances. (Any of that work as a quote?)"

Publishers want endorsements from other writers, possible blurbs from names that readers will recognize. A long-time acquaintance, film director and producer Martin Scorsese, provided a substantial endorsement of an academic novel I wrote: "*Final Exam* dazzles from the first page and intrigues from the first shrewd twist of its plot. It is a superb mystery novel..."

Sometimes your neighbors help out. Daniel Mark Epstein, the poet, dramatist, and biographer, lives just a few blocks from me. For *A Call From Jersey*, he wrote: "P.F. Kluge has enchanting powers: a narrative voice that is distinctive without being mannered, and fictional characters bold to express their deepest emotions without sentimentality..."

And there are writers you only know by reputation who do you a kindness. Novelist Sherman Alexie, author of *The Absolutely True Diary of a Part-Time Indian*, wrote an introduction for *Eddie and the Cruisers*. Sterling Seagrave, author of the *Soong Dynasty*, blurbed *MacArthur's Ghost*. And the late James Michener, author of *Hawaii*, was very generous in his praise: "*The Edge of Paradise* is a responsible, poetic, perceptive look at an American problem that will not go away – what our national posture should be regarding the many islands of Micronesia. P.F. Kluge, with his trenchant observations as a Peace Corps volunteer a quarter of a century ago and his review of Micronesian history on recent return trips, gives a glowing account of the beauty of the islands, the tenacity of their citizens and the complexity that engulfs well-intentioned leaders who try to govern the islands...Both instructive and pleasurable, *The Edge of Paradise* recalled for me many exciting days in those islands and told me things I had not known."

THE BUSINESS OF WRITING
Reviews

L ike any writer, I hope that my readers can engage with my subjects and with the personalities that populate my books. What one hopes for is a glowing review that demonstrates that you delivered.

"As a piece of writing, *The Edge of Paradise* is a brilliant achievement; as analysis it is equally successful. Unlike the instant expert, Kluge does not presume to have the last word. He's been there long enough and often enough to know that everything is hopelessly tangled, fathomlessly deep, and that no mortal, especially a foreigner, can ever know the truth – only a version that makes sense to him, for a while, maybe."

– Ronald Wright, *The Washington Post*, May 1991

"That voice – jaundiced, seasoned, amused, and vibrant as it is – gives *The Master Blaster* added allure. This is not a young man's book; it's the work of a writer who has seen the world, literally and figuratively, for a long time. *The Master Blaster* is tinged with thoughts of mortality, but they are offset by a bon vivant's occasional flash of gratitude and beauty."

– Janet Maslin, *The New York Times*

"P.F. Kluge is a national treasure. His prose is irresistible, and his storytelling is masterly. That's why a new book by him constitutes an event. *The Williamson Turn* is a novel that's a voyage on many levels, including a passage into ourselves, whoever we may be, and the final port of call is pure wonder."

– Joseph Di Prisco,
author of *The Pope of Brooklyn* and *Subway to California*

"Like D.H. Lawrence, he (Kluge) has a keen ear for dialogue, an ability to make what is alien seem exotic, and a fascination with societies in turmoil. The latter no doubt attracted him to the Marcos-era Philippines, which serves as the setting for his fourth book, *MacArthur's Ghost*.

– David DeVoss, *Los Angeles Times*, Dec 13, 1987

"P.F. Kluge, the author of *Eddie and the Cruisers*, writes lyrically, whether he's describing the gaudy onstage triumphs of his Elvis trinity or the crushing hardships of life around the Subic Bay naval base. And he links the stages of Big E's life to what he sees as the phases of America's identity…*Biggest Elvis* is a "dreamy, melancholy tale of economic and pop-cultural imperialism."

– Sarah Ferguson, *The New York Times*, July 5, 1996

"P.F. Kluge, the author of *Season for War*, wields the pen with power, relating events almost ignored by history books, facets of war and the soldiers who fight that astound and disturb... Kluge has the ability to evoke scenes that give the reader a sense of participating in the events portrayed. He brings life to his protagonist and to the members of the 25th Cavalry while raising questions about the morality of war..."

– Lynn Eckman, *Roanoke Times and World News*, May 26, 1986

THE BUSINESS OF WRITING
Bookstores

It's not hard to get your hands on a book. They can be borrowed from libraries, ordered by mail, rescued from yard or estate sales. People don't take their libraries with them when they die. They leave their books behind on bookshelves or in piles at the end of the driveway.

I encourage obtaining books from whatever source one chooses. But my preference is a bookstore, one with a seasoned staff and a selection of books that express the tastes and background of the patrons who support it. Among my favorites is the Strand Bookstore, a prime vendor in New York City, which has been selling books since 1927. It has 18 miles of books, 2.5 million new and used. The books are where they ought to be and staffers assist in the searches that get tricky.

On the ground floor, just inside the front door of the Strand are tables of bestsellers and stacks of new books proclaiming success in the battle for attention and praise. Many appear to be review copies, books that have been sent to book reviewers with the hope of a public recommendation and praise. Some of those stacks of new releases, it appears, never made it to a reviewer. They were sent to a book vendor, or maybe directly to the Strand, for sale on the new releases table. That's what the evidence suggests when the publisher's press release and author's photo are tucked among unread pages.

The Strand is one of a kind. Most readers head for
Barnes & Noble, if they are lucky enough to live near
one. Barnes & Noble is a dependable bookstore though
there are fewer stores all the time. And in those stores
that remain, the spaces for books are being squeezed
by more and more non-book items, tote bags, greeting
cards, daily planners. Still, I am grateful for Barnes &
Noble, which encourages browsing, discoveries and
impulsive decisions.

Where Barnes & Noble falls short is its attention to
special and rare books like those one discovers in places
like Powell's, a wonderful bookstore in Portland, Oregon,
where there is 1.6 acres of retail floor space and four
million new, used, rare and out of print books. This is a
bookstore business that buys 3,000 used books a day.

But most readers never visit these iconic booksellers
in New York or Oregon. If they are lucky, they have a
neighborhood bookstore, a one-of-a-kind store, often
small. These are places where like the bar on the television show *Cheers*, everybody knows your name.

While I'm not likely to be recognized at the Strand or
at Powell's, I am known at BookEnds, a bookstore in
Kailua, Hawaii, a bookshop about one quarter the size of
a Barnes & Noble. Still, on floor-to-ceiling shelves, there
are perhaps 60,000 books. This is a bookstore where a
reader makes special discoveries with the guidance of Pat
Banning, BookEnds' owner. On any given day she sells
up to 300 books.

Pat was a French and journalism major in college, with no
intention of becoming a bookseller. But when she moved

to Hawaii she took a job as a book buyer, primarily for children's books, at a bookstore in Ala Moana, a Honolulu shopping mall. When she learned that the Honolulu Book Shop, on the other side of the island of Oahu, was going out of business, "I bought myself a job," she said. That was 1998. Since then Pat has been her own boss. She manages the store, chooses the books, deals with vendors and with those folks cleaning out their libraries. And, she befriends and encourages writers.

Among a row of authors in alphabetical order I find four of my books, which may be an honor or an embarrassment, since they are shockingly unsold. But, I decide that I'm in good order, alphabetically at least, just behind Stephen King.

A bookstore like BookEnds compliments the town. When I am there I feel among friends, others who – like me – prefer holding the book, turning the pages, touching the paper and sometimes making a note in the margin.

I am not against other ways to access books, whether on Kindle, Books on Tape or the growing number of other ways information is delivered. I admit I am thankful for the marketing sophistication of publishers and bookstores, which will get you what you want in whatever form that encourages you to read. And, I don't mind that my reading preferences are tracked, and that through book club memberships I can stay up to date on trends and new authors. In fact, I have a version of a personal book shopper. As a gift, a former student gave me a membership to Brilliant Books, which likes to call itself "Your Long Distance Local Bookstore."

I am lucky to live in a college town with a bookstore and library. And, in the next town, there's a good independent bookstore, a library and a library warehouse, a huge former factory at the edge of town. I call it the Book Barn. It has well organized shelves and volunteers who are helpful and often entertaining. Every year, I donate several boxes of books. In exchange, though I restrict myself, I select a few books to take home.

THE PEACE CORPS IS GOING TO PARADISE

"The Peace Corps sent me to Micronesia.
I owe them for that."

THE PEACE CORPS IS
GOING TO PARADISE
The First Novel

"Peace Corps volunteers – who learn our languages and cultures, who live amongst us and with us as family – remain, by an order of magnitude, the best bridge at uniting peoples and promoting peace."
– David W. Panuelo, President, the Federated States of Microniesia (FSM), September 2022

My first novel, that first test of my talent, was published in 1976, less than ten years after I'd completed a Ph.D. at the University of Chicago and where, still young enough to be drafted and possibly sent to Vietnam, I took the advice of a professor, who encouraged me to apply to the Peace Corps.

When I applied, I had in mind a destination that was exotic, a place like Ethiopia. But when my acceptance letter arrived I was assigned to Micronesia, a group of islands in the northern Pacific that the U.S. acquired after World War II. The Trust Territory of the Pacific Islands was U.S. territory. They spoke English, spent dollars, were becoming a democracy and a valuable strategic base from which to monitor Asia.

I was assigned in 1967 to the Trust Territory headquarters and given the job of reporting, writing and editing the *Micronesian Reporter*, a magazine that chronicled the

U.S.'s involvement and interest in the region. It gave me the resources and the authority to travel the islands and to interview current and future leaders.

It was the beginning of decades of engagement in the Pacific, which included my return to Saipan in 1975 at a critical point in the creation of the Federated States of Micronesia. Less than a decade after I first saw the islands, I was a director of the Constitutional Convention and the author of the Preamble to the Constitution.

The Day That I Die, my first novel, was published in 1976 by Bobbs Merrill. It was set in Micronesia.

THE PEACE CORPS IS GOING TO PARADISE
Micronesia

"...eventually you worry about staying too long."

The Peace Corps sent me to Micronesia in 1967. Saipan, Mariana Islands, was my home for two years. The experience influenced my life, gave me characters, topics, and a territory. Like many Peace Corps Volunteers I considered staying in the islands. I did not. But I have returned many times. And, on one of those early trips, for *GEO Magazine*, I wrote about my Peace Corps island of Saipan.

There has always been something sad about the Marianas. They are not beautiful palm-fringed atolls with curling coral reefs and bright turquoise lagoons. With more cliffs than beaches, more clumps of scrub pine and brush than palm trees, these islands are rocky places, the tops of volcanoes that emerged from the oceanic depths near the Marianas Trench. They are formidable, masculine, handsome. And sad.

Perhaps the sadness began in 1521, when Magellan came across these Micronesian islands and christened them Islas de los Landrones (Isles of Thieves) because of the pilfering natives. Or when the Spaniards who followed him obliterated, one way or another, more than 90 percent of the original inhabitants and bred with the rest, thus diluting what they did not destroy of the native Chamoro culture. Or perhaps the sadness is more of recent origin, stemming from the time at the end of the Spanish-American War when the links of the island chain were cut, the U.S. acquiring Guam while Germany took over the Northern Marianas – Saipan, Tinian, Rota, and 11 other islands. And the sadness surely did not lift under World War I, when Japan was granted a League of Nations mandate to rule the former German colonies, nor after World War II, when America assumed stewardship over the entire chain.

The 17,000 people of the Marianas have learned to acquiesce, to submit to the foreigners who have dominated their history. The only question now is whether they have judged the current tide correctly. They have voted – and the U.S. Congress has agreed – that the islands will become a permanent part of the United States. Sometimes in the next few years, the islanders will become American citizens. The troubled times, some say, are finally over. The past is history.

Innocents' Progress
A Peace Corps veteran looks back at his –
and America's – ties to Micronesia

By Tony Gibbs, *ISLANDS Magazine*

When 25-year-old P.F. Kluge emerged from the University of Chicago in 1967, Ph.D. in hand, the Peace Corps seemed his inevitable next step. But he could scarcely have been more contemptuous about his intended haven from the Vietnam-era military draft: "A children's crusade...an act of missionary arrogance," was how he saw it, as he recalls in *The Edge of Paradise: America in Micronesia* (Random House), his eloquent reconstruction of his experiences meshed with two decades of the islands' history.

Kluge was one of a relative deluge of Peace Corps volunteers who arrived in Micronesia (900 of them, compared to 65 for all of India) with the announced mission of reversing 20 years of administrative neglect, while participating in the natives' lifestyle. The newcomers were ready for the hostility they got from the territory's staff, a collection of "ex-marines, cashiered politicos, exiled bureaucrats, research anthropologists, miscellaneous island lovers," and a few elite Micronesians. But the high moral ground was cut from under the volunteers by what Kluge calls "the crushing lesson: *Voluntary poverty did not impress.* 'Living on the level of the people' came off as naïve, as downright wacky, when it was from that level people were trying to escape."

Kluge, in contrast to his colleagues, had a relatively cushy berth in the trust territory capital on Saipan, where he edited a quarterly magazine. Micronesia gradually insinuated itself under his skin – partly he told *ISLANDS* in a recent interview, because the island felt like "a penetrable mystery." Even so, it seemed likely that he would finish his two-year hitch as coolly detached as when he arrived. Then he interviewed a young Palauan named Lazarus Salii, a graduate of the University of Hawaii and a budding politician. Their encounter was merely businesslike, and Kluge, at least, had no reason to think more would come of it.

Not long afterward, however, Salii became head of the territory's Future Political Status Commission, the group that was considering Micronesia's wide-open political horizon: Once the U.S. trusteeship ended, the trust territory might become a U.S. commonwealth, like Puerto Rico, or a territory, like nearby Guam. It might seek outright annexation or statehood. And there was always the intoxicating urge toward independence. Salii asked Kluge to draft a statement of intent for the committee, something "sexy and eloquent, a way of capturing the United States' attention."

The task fired Kluge's imagination. He quickly punched out a manifesto, in which the Micronesians asked for what they called a free association with the United States: The islanders would have virtual independence, including the right to end the arrangement, and be given financial support in return for allowing American military bases.

"Never before, never since, have I seen anything I'd written so please a reader," Kluge says. He was invited to accompany Salii on a tour of the islands designed to sell the concept to the people. "Those next weeks stayed with me for years. Looking back on them, I think they were what Peace Corps service should have been like. For that matter, they were what writing, politics, life itself should be: the close-up knowledge, the behind-the-scenes struggles, the passionate campaign…" It was the beginning of a 20-year association between the two men, a relationship that would end in tragedy, and produce this chronicle of what happened to the islands, to Salii and other would-be statesmen, to Kluge himself.

Kluge's Peace Corps enlistement ended in 1969 and he went back to the United States, became a journalist and, later, a novelist. He married, but part of his heart was still in Micronesia. The islands, meanwhile, had lost their vision of unity; political fragmentation was the order of the day, and the former leaders grabbed what they could from the shambles. Salii's own career seemed to peak when he became the second president of the Republic of Palau, a not-quite-nation happily mired in the spoils system.

As old friendships will, the relationship between the American writer and the Micronesian wheeler-dealer faded, kept alive by occasional phone calls. And then, in August 1988, came the shocking news: Salii had put a bullet through his head. Kluge, teaching in Ohio at Kenyon College, felt history rush in on him. He realized that his life's most memorable period needed a proper summation, and that his friend's apparently reasonless suicide was not it.

Like a good novel, *The Edge of Paradise* is readable on several levels – as popular history, seen through acid-etched glasses; as what Kluge today calls "an attempt to do justice to that imperfect life"; as an informed travelogue of places seen from inside and out simultaneously. It is a long and complex story, illuminated by the author's perceptions as much as by his obsession with the telling phrase (and, sometimes, the telling catalog).

Much of Kluge's best writing in *The Edge of Paradise* is constructed around a carefully burnished cynicism. But under every cynic's armor beats an idealist's often bruised yet ever hopeful heart, and Kluge is no exception. Having quoted so many of his cutting observations, it seems fair to balance the equation with a ringing affirmation: "What I am starting to believe is that an island doesn't belong only to the people who are born on it or who claim the right to own – or sell – it. An island belongs to the people who think and care about it, though they cast no votes and own no land. That is the sovereignty of the heart. Everything else is money and noise."

Never Quite Making Peace
With the U.S. Peace Corps

By P.F. Kluge
The New York Times

Evanston, Illinois – There are two kinds of American college seniors, I have noticed. Some have their lives planned before graduation. Eyes ahead, forward march. You hope they get what they want – only not too easily.

I have a weakness for the other ones, who emerge from four years at a liberal arts college wondering what next. Those are the ones who ask about the Peace Corps. Their question gives me more trouble than they know.

When I think of my Peace Corps years – Micronesia in the late 1960s – I think of a time and place that are gone from me now, and a younger self gone, too. My loyalty, curiosity, nostalgia run to islands named Saipan and Palau, not to the U.S. agency that sent me there.

When the invitation to celebrate the Peace Corps's 30th anniversary in Washington arrived, I hesitated. I noticed that the Peace Corps had not lost its knack for devising ceremonies that could turn out to be poignant or, maybe, embarrassing. There is to be a commemorative parade, volunteers marching behind the flag of the country they served in, and a "living world map" a kind of *tableau vivant*.

There is also Volunteer Day, which will be spent cleaning up rivers, planting trees, painting and repairing the houses of the poor. No Peace Corps occasion is complete, I guess, unless we have spent time working for nothing. It comes back to me now, what I used to resent: the whiff of strenuous virtue.

I have never quite made my peace with the Peace Corps. It has to do with the matter of using, and getting used, and it came in three stages.

First, we had to wonder whether we weren't being used by our government. This was especially true in Micronesia, which the United States had captured in World War II and had administered ever since. The United States needed to win hearts and minds.

The Peace Corps program in Micronesia was one of the most publicized – and the largest: 900 volunteers for a population that could be comfortably seated in the Rose Bowl. So we worried about being used, how and by whom.

The Peace Corps should never follow the flag too closely. But on Saipan, where I was based, editing a magazine, it was flapping right overhead.

The second issue was more troubling: the crushing discovery that living on the level of the people can come off as downright wacky to the people who want to escape that level.

We learned local languages while teaching English to the locals. Fair enough – but what we found was that, while hoping to meet a culture on its own terms, we participated in its transformation and, quite possibly, its destruction.

We lived like locals, yes, but they wanted to live like us (who could blame them?) – and they used us to that end. They may have been touched by our willingness to come, but they ached for our ability to leave.

After leaving, though, the third and final wonder dawned. Were we users too? I got more than I gave. I have never met a Peace Corps volunteer who doesn't agree.

It is good news, I suppose, a plus for us, knowing that our temporary largesse was far outweighed by the courtesy and forbearance we received.

But after you left you wondered how you looked to the people you left behind, whether you were part of anything more than a one-sided exchange of citizens.

It won't go away, my problem with the Peace Corps.

What do I say to this college senior sitting in my office savoring her last, safe, mellow campus springtime, pondering a couple years in Botswana? Or maybe – amazingly – Eastern Europe. (Who will be the first Peace Corps volunteer who sends home a postcard beginning "Last year in Marienbad…"?)

Should I burden her with reservations now? Hedge her adventure with Micronesian ironies?

Micronesia comes back to me all the time: the scar on my left arm from the night I slept too close to a mosquito coil; the way metal roofs expand at dawn, contract sighingly at dusk: a certain kind of heat, green and hothouse heavy; a certain kind of rain, shifting from drizzle to cascade in a minute.

The Peace Corps sent me to Micronesia: I owe them for that.

My student may wonder why she's going. While she's away she may wonder what she's doing. Later she may wonder why she's leaving or what it meant.

Never mind. There are worse mistakes. I tell her to go.

—

The writer, a novelist, is author of *The Edge of Paradise: America in Micronesia*. He contributed this comment to *The New York Times*.

THE WRITER

THE WRITER
My Islands

My nonfiction list is short, two books. One is about Micronesia. The second is about Kenyon College. The subjects may seem to be very different, but they share common characteristics. They are islands.

I write about places where I've lived and worked. My nonfiction is personal. I know the people I write about. I've known them for years. I know the leaders, the histories, the aspirations and the mistakes. I am an insider. But while my journalistic skills are useful, I write for the sake of history.

The nonfiction I've written remains in print largely because the books are historical markers against which current realities can be measured. My Micronesia engagement, for example, spans decades.

I first went to Micronesia in 1967 and lived there for two years. I returned to the islands in 1975 for six months. Since then, I've made two dozen trips, maybe more to Palau, the southern-most island group in Micronesia. I've seen changes in leadership, young radicals grown old, new investors with foreign deals and a welcomed national effort to save Palau's extraordinary environment.

NONFICTION
MICRONESIA

NONFICTION – MICRONESIA

"There is no encounter, no adventure, no love,
no defeat or victory that would not be lost
were it not recorded."

When I visit Palau, I try to get out to the outer islands, which are still beautiful and wonderfully quiet. On one of these trips, I began to realize how important my book, *The Edge of Paradise*, is to Palauans.

PAGE 6

I wrote about a trip to Peleliu in an article titled *PAGE 6*:

I caught a ride on a boat from Koror, Palau's main city, down to the island of Peleliu, site of a prolonged and costly battle that cost 1,800 American lives, the most fatal amphibious assault in U.S. history. Almost all of the 30,000 Japanese defenders perished in what was probably an unnecessary battle. Douglas MacArthur felt his return to the Philippines might be jeopardized by the Japanese on Peleliu. He was wrong. The Japanese lacked offensive capacity, planes and ships. But, as the Americans discovered, they could fight and die. A battle that was supposed to be over in a few days took months.

What I liked about Peleliu is that it lacks the usual battlefield trappings, guides, maps, signs. It's a battlefield that's been left behind, left alone and it invites personal discovery of rusted tanks, an overgrown landing strip, gun emplacements, caves and tunnels.

After roaming around, I am invited to check in with the island's governor, Temmy Shmull. He sits behind his desk. It feels like he's been waiting for me. We've barely said hello when he looks down at a book lying on his desk. "Page Six," he announces and begins to read... "Farther south is Peleliu, island of Bloody Nose Ridge, rusted landing craft and war-littered caves famed for the savagery of the battle fought between Japanese and Americans during World War II and, more recently, for the high quality of its marijuana, grown in sawed-off oil barrels., smuggled to Guam in Styrofoam coolers, in hollowed-out baseball bats, in the bellies of frozen fish." Governor Shmull looks up at me. "Page Six," he repeats. He's smiling and my concern fades. He's been reading from a book I wrote twenty-five years ago, *The Edge of Paradise*, an account of my experience in the islands and, also, an elegy for a dead friend. The book sold decently in the U.S. In Palau, it was – and remains – important. And here I confront a pleasing truth. Palau, a place that I remember, is a place that remembers me.

I met my first Palauans on Saipan, which was headquarters of the U.S. administered Trust Territory of the Pacific Islands, a swath of some 2,000 islands which – as every article I wrote inevitably declared – included six distinct districts, nine languages, a land mass that amounted to half the size of Rhode Island, scattered over an area equivalent to the 48 states and a population that could fit into the Pasadena Rose Bowl. There were the Marshalls, Kusai (later Kosrae), Ponape (later Pohnpei), Truk (later Chuuk), the Northern Marianas, Yap and Palau.

The Palauans were impressive. They held a dispro-
portionate number of government jobs, they ran the
best bars, they were ready to talk – to argue. They had
opinions. In other places, straightforward questions got
"maybe" responses. In Palau it was "yes" or "no." The
Palauans were quick to size you up, to figure an angle.
Who was this American? What did he do? What could
he do for them? Palau was someplace I could not miss,
they insisted. They seemed to think it was the center of
the world. And, before long, I agreed.

At the time I showed up, Palau was facing crucial
decisions. They'd survived colonization. The Spanish
came for god, their saying went, the Germans for
glory, the Japanese for gold and the American – an
edgy double-entendre here – for good. As a Peace
Corps journalist, editing a magazine, the *Micronesia
Reporter*, I met island leaders. I published a long-
ish interview in question and answer format with
Lazarus Salii, a Palauan who worked at Trust Territory Headquarters and soon left to embark on a
political career back home. He was brilliant, funny,
moody, a tumultuous mix. And we clicked. I wrote
speeches that he delivered at the United Nations, I
wrote proposals and articles and manifestos. What
Ted Sorenson did for JFK, I did for Lazarus. Our
partnership meant a lot to me. After Palau became
a republic, he was elected president. Then, in the
late eighties, things got complicated. Near the end
of his first term he called me. I was in Manhattan.
He wanted me to come to Palau. When? As soon as
possible. To do what? We'd work that out. I had a
job in New York, I said, I could not leave right away.
The call was inconclusive.

When I thought about him, it seemed his career repli-
cated that of three U.S. presidents. He was Kennedy at
the start – purposeful, impressive, lively. Then he was
LBJ, wheeling and dealing adroitly. Towards the end,
he was Nixon, compromised and entangled. Nixon
resigned. Lazarus Salii went beyond that. At home
one afternoon, at a time when he was a cinch to be
re-elected, Lazarus Salii put a bullet in his head. That
late night phone call – that plea – he made to me suggested he wanted me to remind him of his younger
self. I let him down. One of my life's great friendships
had ended. But Palau remained.

Now, when I return to Palau I know where to go,
before I check into a hotel, before I say hello to
anyone. My wife and I drive through town to where
the road ends at a place called Icebox, where we can
park and contemplate Palau's great attraction, now a
World Heritage site: The Rock Islands. They begin just
across a narrow channel and go on for miles – dozens,
probably hundreds of coral islets. Undercut by the
sea, they are mushroom-shaped at the bottom, dense-
ly forested and impossible to land on or to climb. As
islands go they are touch-me-nots. See them one at a
time, they are handsome, see them as part of a larger design, they are beautiful. It's as if a creator got
bored with continents and oceans and took time, just
once, to offer a subtle, intricate, equitable partnership
between land and sea, with reefs, channels, coves,
caves and tiny beaches. Paradise, these days, is a word
you use carefully; often it invites irony. But this is it.
And the Palauans know it. It's their spiritual retreat, an
escape from crowds, cars, traffic, noise, work, politics
and, maybe, for a little while, ambition.

Back in Koror, I check into a hotel run by Tina Salii, Lazarus' widow. I start running into people. Their greeting is very Palauan. No hug. No smile, no lei or aloha. They spot me and the look on their face is close to a scowl. "When did you come?" they ask. It's the tone of an interrogation. Why was I not informed? And how many days have passed without your contacting me? And how many more, if we hadn't met by accident just now? But I like surprising old friends, lawyers, judges, businessmen, old timers, all happy to get on a boat or go to a restaurant or have another beer. "Talking story" it's called. It's as if I'd followed a show on television, a melodrama, and then gone away. Now I need to be updated. I know the basic story, the setting, the characters… but not what's happened lately, all the twists and turns.

Years ago, all the buzz was about U.S. intentions, possible military bases, CIA spying, for which I was sometimes fingered. Now it's about Chinese invest-ment and tourists. They fear that Palau, along with many other Pacific islands, will become Chinese border towns. That's a concern. But there's a pride in Palau, in being a Palauan, that you see in the way people attend to the elderly, in the way kids carry themselves as they go to school, their way of talking and walking. I like their chances. There's a Palauan expression which is used when you refer to a former intimate, an old flame. "It was." He or she, you might say, is your "it was." Palau is mine, my "it was," and is and will always be.

PRAISE

"Someone you don't know has been paying attention."

Success as a writer can be measured in a number of ways. Books sold. Movie deals contemplated. Guest appearances. Royalty checks cashed. The line outside the doors at a bookstore appearance. But how does this happen? How does the world know about you?

There are scores of brilliant writers never discovered, never lucky enough to make that connection that leads to success. Talent may not be enough. And your assessment of your own talent may not be widely shared.

But sometimes luck plays a role and you discover that someone you don't know has been paying attention. And sometimes that attention leads to insightful criticism and praise.

Praise for *The Edge of Paradise*
By Ronald Wright
The Washington Post

P.F. Kluge, perhaps best known for his novel *Eddie and the Cruisers*, is again investigating a mysterious death. But this time the subject is truth not fiction, and the question is not whether the victim died, but how and why. The dead man's name is Lazarus: Lazarus Salii, president of the Republic of Palau, a baker's dozen of tiny islands somewhere in the western Pacific. On Aug. 20, 1988, Salii was found with a .357 magnum at his feet, a hole in his head and part of his hair "transplanted onto his office wall."

Fred Kluge was Salii's friend; they had known each other half their lives. Back in the '60s, when Kluge was a Peace Corps Volunteer, he had written most of Salii's speeches. He also wrote the loftier bits in the islands' constitution. Micronesia was that kind of place. Kluge thought he was doing good, and he had fun doing it. It was a time "when it seemed that America would leave a clean smell behind." But what kind of place was it in the 1980s? Palau's first president murdered in 1986; its second, Lazarus Salii, killed... how? And was there "any way a big place can touch a little one without harming it?"

Fred Kluge wanted to find out. Partly because Salii was his friend; partly because he wanted to know what had gone wrong since he and a bunch of fellow dreamers and pacifists – "a new kind of American" – went there in 1964. And partly because he wanted to know why he had never been able to stay in Paradise: why an apartment in New York could be home, why those islands he loved could not. And if he had stayed, what then? Would he have been able to talk Lazarus out of suicide, if it was suicide? Would he have been able to save him, if it wasn't?

In Kluge's talented hands, these questions and obsessions become not merely engrossing but acquire archetypal resonance. Who has not paused, in the middle of a life, to contemplate moves, failures, betrayals? Who has not flirted with the Gauguin fantasy – chucking it all and escaping to Paradise? Trouble is, how many of us really know what happened to Gauguin and the rest? Booze, syphilis, morphine, trouble with the police, fights with husbands and fathers… Fred Kluge knows. These islands are his "personal Yokna-patawpha." He knows them for what they are: a blend of "Kmart and Gauguin." His pages drip with sweat and watery beer; the shells on his beach are Budweiser cans, his island nights are filled with noisy mufflers and feigned cries of passion from porno tapes running at top volume on the locals' VCRs. His islanders are bored stiff by palm trees, sunshine and pellucid water. They want to go to Las Vegas; and if they come back to Paradise they want to build Las Vegas there.

Salii liked jet travel and Washington talks at which nothing was ever settled; he "used lawyers like Kleenex." He made plenty of enemies, and perhaps the worst was himself. The brilliant young nationalist became an ardent campaigner for the "Compact of Free Association," an ill-defined form of adhesion to the United States. The anti-nuclear activist spent his last efforts trying to kill the anti-nuke clause in Palau's constitution that he himself had helped to put there years before.

So Kluge goes back, approaching his dead friend by the long route, closing in on an island, something like the way America closed in on Japan: Majuro, Ponape, Truk, Saipan, Yap. Places that sound like the brand names of Bulgarian tractors. The style, like the journey, is episodic – astonishing poetic flights and gritty, beery, Yankee slang.

As a piece of writing *The Edge of Paradise* is a brilliant achievement; as analysis it is equally successful. Unlike the instant expert, Kluge does not presume to have the last word. He's been there long enough and often enough to know that everything is hopelessly tangled, fathomlessly deep, and that no mortal, especially a foreigner, can ever know the truth – only a version that makes sense to him, for a while maybe. In short, he's learned his island lessons: "that everything is connected, that everybody is related, that no change is permanent…that means matter more than ends, and are more fun too, that rumor beats truth…that people matter more than principles…Palauans matter more than foreigners…and some Palauans matter more than other Palauans. That's where things get tricky.

By the way, how did Lazarus die? Perhaps you've guessed. But somehow that isn't the point. Getting there – in this sensitive, subtle, and superbly written book – that's the point.

NONFICTION
EDUCATION

NONFICTION EDUCATION

"If you're a writer, nothing is ever over until it is written down."

I now live in Gambier, Ohio. I can see the dorm where I lived as a student from the front porch of my home. I lived in Lewis Hall, an all-male dormitory. And that's where I returned to live and research *Alma Mater: A College Homecoming*, a month-by-month honest report of a year in the life of a liberal arts college. Some loved it. Others had objections. In the end, the book is quoted in college recruitment videos, read by educators and administrators and quoted widely. The book got me national attention and special notice in *The New York Times*.

A Writer's College Homecoming
The New York Times, April 10, 1994
By P.F. Kluge

Writing about a college is like writing about your parents while they are still alive. I was warned about this from the beginning, warned that love and loyalty wouldn't help once I attempted a nonfiction account of a year at Kenyon College, my alma mater, my current employer. It was a no-win proposition, a kamikaze flight, an untenured professor's invitation to his own career suicide. And an irresistible idea.

How many books have attempted to capture the deep traditions, the insular tensions, the seasonal wars that characterize life at a small American liberal arts college? Who has bothered to record the compromises and betrayals, the wonderful mix of seriousness and silliness? Jarrell, Lurie, McCarthy, Malamud, Malone – I could name a handful of books, not enough for even the skimpiest syllabus – they focused on personal issues and decaying marriages more than on the life of the institution. All those readers, yet so few writers. Something seems to get in their way.

I spent a full year at Kenyon, in Gambier, Ohio, putting myself in the way of as much experience as possible. I lived in the same freshman dorm I'd occupied 30 years before, lectured and graded, sometimes exhilarated, sometimes in despair. Kenyon had its good and bad days and so did I. I followed hiring searches, faculty debates, alumni complaints, admissions meetings. The book that results, *Alma Mater: A College Home-*

coming, was mixed. How could it be otherwise? You could find evidence in it that Kenyon College was a good, occasionally excellent place, with a prudent administration, able faculty, lively student body. A place worth defending. But that wasn't the whole truth. Some other passages discovered a thin-skinned place, complacent, fractious and adrift, in need of shaping up.

I tried to tell the truth and I tried to be fair, to pick, if not pull, my punches. In the end, it would have been easy to write a book that was harsher and it would have been hard to write a book that was gentler. But that was my opinion. There were other opinions, as I discovered when I came back to campus in January.

I've always enjoyed returning, as a teacher, to the college where I once was taught. And little Gambier is wonderful even at its bleakest, at the start of second semester, sullen and ominous, a time of salt-stained streets and slushy lawns, gray hillsides and May a light-year away. Perched on an Ohio hilltop, surrounded by farms and scraps of forest, brushed by a river spanned by rusting railroad trestles, Kenyon is the very image of a small residential college, a perfect intersection of thought and growth and haunting memory. But this year I came back worried, like a teenager creeping home late at night, parking a just-dented family car in the garage, tiptoeing upstairs and waiting for hard questions – or pained silences – at the breakfast table.

My absence during first semester had spared me the college's immediate reaction to *Alma Mater*, which appeared in late November. The student newspaper interviewed Kenyon's president, whose public response was polite, if strained: "The critical temper is not surprising since there must be shadows and bright spots to make the book plausible." The dean of admissions declared the book "incomplete or not well rounded" and a student who "forked over the equivalent of three 10-inch sausage, pineapple and cheddar cheese pizzas" to buy my book pronounced herself well satisfied. In early December, hundreds of students and faculty packed into Philomathesian Hall, a dark wood lecture hall with stained glass windows, for a campus-wide forum on my book. The meeting seems to have been a mix of damage control, celebration, group therapy and in-absentia trial.

Later, listening to a bootleg tape, blurry and indistinct, I feel as if I'm eavesdropping on a jury room. I am criticized, I am generously defended. I am "brutal but honest," one voice declares, I am Kenyon's "somewhat disappointed lover," said another. Somebody – could my ears be deceiving me? – compares me to J.D. Salinger. Others, no doubt, are picturing Benedict Arnold.

Soon after, reports started coming in from outside: concern among Kenyon parents, prospective donors up in arms, irate alumni sniffing treason. "Are we going to rescind the s.o.b.'s degree?" one old-timer inquired.

The wisest decision, I supposed, would have been not to return at all. That's the writer's usual pattern. You research and report, you immerse yourself, indiscriminately, because anything might be material. Then you

withdraw to write. And when that's over your withdrawal becomes an escape, even if it's only to another book. But I returned to Gambier to witness the
consequences of my writing, the judgement of my
judgements, my work worked over.

"I'm surprised they let you back in town," joked a college security officer when he saw me on my first night
back. "Are you working on your resume?" inquired a
former student. "Have you seen the president yet?"
"Have you talked to the president's wife?" Those
questions set the pattern, a probing, almost prurient
interest that was less about the book than about its
impact on the college, on applications and admissions,
on other people. The issue wasn't whether the book
was good, but whether it was good – or bad – for
Kenyon and for me. The impact of the book is, as
they like to say at colleges, problematic. The college
goes about its work, confronting lower enrollments,
staff reductions, budget cutbacks, increased concern
about the cost of liberal arts education and skepti-
cism about its benefits. It's a time of austerity, anxiety
and anger. "The future will resemble the present...or
worse," Kenyon's president warned a faculty meeting
just the other day.

All of this suggests that here or elsewhere there'll be
plenty of material for other books on college life, and
so I offer some advice to other writers who enter this
green, cloistered arena.

***Think carefully about whether to tell them what
you're up to***. How deliciously tempting it was to
consider writing *Alma Mater* on the sly. I knew from

other years at Kenyon the richness of the material that
would come to me, unsought. Every secret is meant to
be told, sooner or later. At a small campus, you don't
have to wait so long. But I decided it wouldn't be fair
to ambush Kenyon. I announced my intentions and
lived with the substantial costs.

Some people turned sullen, or skeptical, or strenuously
– unquotably – polite. With others, the opposite happened, and I confronted those statements that hang
in the air like ballooned utterances over the heads of
cartoon characters, statements begging "quote me!
quote me!" And then there were people protecting
their jobs by going "off the record" or "not for attri-
bution," as if we were trading Oval Office secrets in a
Washington parking garage.

Realize that not everyone will admire your work. It
wasn't just what I said about, say, spousal hiring or
grade inflation. My opinions could be discounted as an
old grad's nostalgia, or the meanderings of a part-time
hire, or the glibness of a journalist out of his depth.
But what about the people I quoted and the things
they said about each other? Reporting old battles, I
threatened to start new ones. And what about the people I never mentioned at all? Wouldn't they be hurt the
most? And then there were alumni who wanted only
the best for their alma mater, and that meant reading
only the best. And Kenyon parents, paying more than
$20,000 per year ($80,000 in 2024) to educate their
kids, didn't want their investment devalued. I didn't
mean to dash their hopes, but somebody had to tell
them that quality is a sometime thing, even at good
schools, that we produce wonderful graduates and

amazing goof-offs and that I didn't mean for them to think less of Kenyon but to think more about it.

Acknowledge that trying to be fair about academe is like building a house on an earthquake fault. Every college is a network of factions and fissures, tremors and spasms, shallow and deep. We have people who are delighted to teach and read and others who stress research; some who'd love to stay here forever, others chafing to move on. There are easy graders and there are martinets, professors who aim to humanize the B students of the world – since they're the ones who end up running it – and professors who measure success by the number of A students who get into graduate schools and try, against cruel odds, to become professors.

Some professors are content with the student body – mostly middle class or upper, mostly white – that finds its way here and pays to come. Others press for diversity, change and outreach. Some of my colleagues believe that the continued existence of fraternities at Kenyon is a moral and intellectual affront. Others say that people who find themselves in the middle of rural Ohio have a right to form groups, give parties and do foolish things occasionally.

A Diverse Group

The student body includes superlative kids who struggle for still-elusive A grades and others who settle cheerfully for the ubiquitous B. (No one puts up with C's; these are life-destroying insults.) We have students for whom Kenyon is magic, a life-enhancing experience, and others for whom it's a slapdash passage from summer camp to country club. We have students who love to write, and others who hate to read. I tried to find room for all of them in my book.

But equality had its cost. To some it was a cop-out, sterile and timid. People wanted to see other people gotten – wanted me to see things their way, fire broadsides where they had only sniped, cut my throat where they swallowed their tongues. Get those fraternity drunks, those whining feminists, those crusty political scientists, those radical-chic historians, that suave, smooth-talking president, that dithering provost. But I used thumb tacks in a place that wanted nails.

In the end, though, it was worth it. People's welcoming reactions – not that they agreed with every point – overwhelmed the hostile. There were letters from today's students and those of 30 years ago. This from a student I don't know, studying overseas this year: "What happens at Kenyon occurs everywhere but is magnified 100 times at a community-oriented institution because every action is taken personally. I hope that I will see you around next year, but if not, good book." Another student said, "You captured the Kenyon I love, and the Kenyon I know, and the Kenyon I want the college to become."

I've heard from teachers and administrators, some still here, others who've moved on to other places and who look back at Kenyon, sometimes with hurt, sometimes affection, often both. Just lately there've been letters from people at other institutions who assure me that Kenyon's problems, and virtues, are not unique. Late afternoons and weekends, hiding in my office, I'm greeted by people who want to talk – total strangers who drive to this small Ohio village to see the special place I wrote about.

A Sense of Connection

The best thing about writing about a real place – and returning to face the consequences – is the sense of connection between your work and your audience. Five books precede *Alma Mater*, and the story was always the same: some reviews, modest sales, a rapid withdrawal from the shelves where books last no longer than a cup of yogurt in a supermarket. Working on the next book, revving up energy and hopes for a new project, I've been haunted by the fate of my earlier efforts.

This time was different: the meetings, the talk, the body English, the hugs and stares, and glares, the letters and gossip, the 700 copies sold in the college bookstore and the first-time chance that, at least in this part of Ohio, a book of mine will outlive its author. Any book is an act of caring and a kind of tribute. It's a gift. It distinguishes its subject from all unremarked places, the ones that never get written about at all. Maybe your college – your parents – will understand it. Maybe they won't. If not today, maybe tomorrow.

2024

Kenyon College is 200-years-old this year and my house, an original dorm built by the college's founder, Philander Chase, is a place of celebration.

Yes, I survived the impact of *Alma Mater*, which became extensively quoted and was used in a multi-million-dollar college fundraising campaign. Passages from the book were read by Academy Award winner Allison Janney, class of 1982, in an emotion-grabbing video.

The book still sells well and people I don't know come to my house to have it autographed. I have an impressive stack of correspondence from college administrators who confirm that they share my experiences. Parents thank me for giving them an inside look. Former students, even those who graduated recently, say the book is still a valid guide.

In my years at Kenyon, good things happened. A grateful student endowed the Kluge Fund, which encourages good student journalism. And, there is a large wood-paneled conference room/classroom, which can be used for social gatherings. It has a balcony overlooking a wooded hill. It's called the P.F. Kluge and Pamela Hollie Seminar Room. And, following my retirement, I received an honorary degree.

In 2022, a new endowed chair was created. It is the Pamela G. Hollie Chair, Global Issues. With a gift of $2.5 million, a former student honored her life's work and her contributions to Kenyon, though she was never a professor and is not a graduate of the college. Pamela is the first minority and the first woman to be honored with an endowed chair at Kenyon.

And yes, we will be buried in the college's cemetery. We'll be around forever.

FICTION

"From things that have happened and from all things that you know and all those you cannot know, you make something through your invention that is not a representation but a whole new thing truer than anything true and alive, and you make it alive, and if you make it well enough, you give it immortality. That is why you write and for no other reason..." – Ernest Hemingway

FICTION

"A journalist writes about what did happen.
A novelist writes about what could happen."

Moving from newspaper and magazine articles to books, is there a greater gamble? Newspapers have a strict format with little room for artistic flourishes. Magazines allow for more creativity, but space is limited and an editor runs the show. A journalist cannot invent situations or characters or control the narrative. So, moving from journalism to fiction is not as easy as it might look. It's a change of gear. It is a truth that haunts journalists, and others, who have a novel-in-progress in the bottom desk drawer, possibly keeping company with a bottle of whiskey. Secret weakness and secret ambition.

I began to write fiction after *LIFE* magazine folded and my next job called for extensive travel to American prisons where I conducted interviews and wrote stilted reports. I was quickly bored. I'm not the kind of writer who writes reports. So, unhappy with the job, I began to consider my options. And on a rainy day, in a nondescript motel near a race track not far from a prison I'd visited, I started to write.

The result was *The Day That I Die*, subtitled "A Novel of Suspense." The book is set in Palau on the World War II battlefield of Peleliu, a rough rocky island riddled with caves, tunnels, rusted war weapons and bitter memories. In the novel, a World War II veteran returns to Peleliu and is murdered. The book, my first published novel, did not make a lot of money or make me famous, but it did give me confidence and it encouraged me to keep writing.

A note: To call yourself a writer, you've got to sell your work. Unlike journalism, there are no assignments from an editor. No guarantee that your work will be published. You are on your own. And it's up to you to convince a publisher that you've created something commercial, something of literary value.

A second note: If you publish your own work, then it's easy to get published. But, self-publishing seldom gets a writer much recognition. Frankly, it is not easy to get published. You are competing with established writers who have agents and contracts and a track record. What's more, just because your first commercial book gets published doesn't mean your next one will be published. There's no guarantee that the second book, or any other book you write, will be automatically accepted, published, paid for, reviewed or promoted. Writing is a gamble.

Eddie and the Cruisers became the proof that I could write a commercial book. It is set in New Jersey, my home state. Because I am of the Rock and Roll generation, I was aware of what happened to the Crickets after Buddy Holly died. In *Eddie and the Cruisers*, the lead singer, Eddie, dies, and the band struggles to survive. The plot involves missing music tapes that could be valuable.

The book found an audience. But, it was not until it was made into a film that the book attracted attention. Those who saw the film noted a glaring difference between the book and the film. In the book, Eddie is dead. In the movie, he's alive.

A third note: When people ask whether movie-makers change the books they turn into films, my retort is: "If you sell a cow to a butcher does he change it?"

A fourth note: I write about places my life, or my wife's, take me to. I don't invent fictional (or fictitious) situations that are too far from the truth. So there is truth in my fiction, things I discover mixed with things I imagine. My fiction owes its truth to real experience. That accounts for three novels that are set in the Philippines, where my wife worked for the *The New York Times* and later for the Asia Foundation. I have been in and out of the Philippines since the 1980's.

My first Philippine novel, *Season For War* (1984) takes place when America asserted itself after the Spanish American War; *MacArthur's Ghost* (1987) takes place in the aftermath of World War II, and *Biggest Elvis* (1996) – my favorite – takes place at the time when the United States military muscle in the Pacific was evident. Two large military bases housed thousands of young American soldiers in the Philippines. During those years, roughly a century after the Spanish American War, Manila had a reputation for fun-and-games nightlife. In my opinion, one book reviewer summed up *Biggest Elvis* perfectly: "Part mystery, part love story, part mordant commentary on America's waning presence, this hugely entertaining novel tells the story of a trio of Elvis impersonators working at a club called Graceland in Olongapo, Philippines. But there are some who think that Biggest Elvis has to go and Biggest Elvis himself senses that something ominous is coming."

A fifth note: Like many writers, I write about things I feel passionate about. One of those topics is education, especially liberal arts education. When I was invited to teach at Kenyon, the village and the college became characters.

Final Exam (2003) is an account of lives and deaths at a college resembling Kenyon. For this novel, I used first person narrators to achieve a mix of voices and attitudes. Unintentionally, I'd written a performance piece. And one evening, three Kenyon faculty members acted out the parts in a public performance. The book had local appeal, of course, but it had a larger audience. Director-filmmaker Martin Scorsese publicly praised the book and provided a blurb for the cover.

A second book, *Gone Tomorrow* (2008) explores the life and death, the accomplishments, and the puzzling silence in the life of a writer teaching at a place like Kenyon. From *Gone Tomorrow* : "George Canaris is the first faculty member in half a century whose death merited an obituary in *The New York Times*. He was our best-known professor...and a mystery."

It's difficult to choose which of my novels is my best. Would you be able to announce a favorite among ten children? In front of those ten kids? No way. But when I'm alone I can make a choice. My choice would be *Gone Tomorrow*. But my second would be the novel, *A Call From Jersey*, because it is the most personal of my novels and because the characters are drawn from my own family history.

My parents came over from Germany in 1924. My father's first job was for an uncle who was the superintendent of an apartment building on 110th Street just north of Central Park in New York City. Onkle (uncle) Bruno brought over a German "greenhorn" every year. My father was one of those greenhorns. My mother, Maria Ensslen, worked as a *fraulein* – a nanny – for German-speaking Jews on the upper West Side of Manhattan. My parents met in the United States.

From the day they arrived, they insisted that they were Americans. And my father, Walter Kluge, insisted that America never let them down.

Around 1950, my parents brought over my father's father, my "opa." But it wasn't long before he indicated that he wanted to go back to Germany. He was grateful for my parent's love and for my affection, but he wanted to go home. America, he granted, was an impressive country. But, he observed, Americans don't know how to work, how to relax or how to eat. He returned to Hamburg.

A Call from Jersey may have the best first line I have ever written: "You couldn't not like Max Schmeling." In the novel, Hans Greifinger, who arrived in the U.S. in 1928, has a son. The son is a travel writer, who changes his last name to Griffin. In reviews of the book, Howard Norman wrote: "This novel is a rare iconic immigrant story – inimitable, mesmerizing, tough-minded, generous and haunting." Another reviewer commented: "Jersey has never seemed more exotic."

Note: Many writers are not comfortable exposing their personal secrets. Others write too much about themselves, using writing as therapy. And yet a story, I feel, profits from a strong dose of reality. That's the journalist in me.

A journalist writes about what did happen. A novelist writes about what could happen.

In *Master Blaster*, a novel, someone on the island of Saipan published, online, controversial investigative information about deals and double dealing. This is dangerous territory for the Master Blaster, who monitors the local government and the island's profiteers. His audience does not know who he is. But one night he's followed by someone identified as X to Suicide Cliff, where, rather than surrender to American forces after WWII, Japanese and Koreans on the island, ignoring pleas to surrender, jumped to their deaths. "Then the Master Blaster did what he'd planned, something learned from the Japanese he'd seen in war footage. He took one backward step not looking at what was or wasn't there. His foot hit the ground. His next step would surely be his last. A second or two in the air, a likely loss of consciousness and a landing that was beyond imagining. He stepped back and on X's face he saw a decision – too late – to stop him. His foot, when it came down, met air. He fell backward and down; below his island awaited him."

Note: Earlier, I stressed the need for a powerful opening. Here in *Master Blaster* is an example of a powerful conclusion. As previously noted: "planes tend to crash on takeoff or on landing."

Some advice: A writer writes, of course. But there's more. There's the editing, but for me, not before I've finished the first draft. A first draft should be full of forays, caprices, experiments: side trips of all kinds. In other words, write it all. Take chances. But do not edit it until the book is done. Sure, I reread and review what is underway. And there's a red light in my head: an alarm that I call my bullshit detector. I do not begin editing before the manuscript is complete. Writing and editing are inevitable. But they should not be simultaneous.

And a couple final thoughts: These are from Tim O'Brien, author of *The Things They Carried*, a book I've taught. On a visit to Kenyon and over a couple of beers, he offered wisdom I appreciated. According to O'Brien, the sense of embellishment, letting one's imagination heighten detail, is part of what fiction writing is about. It's not lying, he said. It's an effort to produce story details which will help to get at a felt experience...
"You tell lies to get at the truth."

FICTION
How Novels are Born

I am often asked where my ideas come from. How do I find the characters? How do I know that the plot will work, or that the subject will interest a reader? More importantly, will the story interest me for the months it will take to produce a book. Many of the ideas come from my travels, from my Peace Corps experience, from my early years in New Jersey and from my last job as Writer-in-Residence at Kenyon College in Ohio. The locations for my novels are as important as the story.

My first novel, *The Day that I Die*, was set in Micronesia, my Peace Corps islands. The second novel, *Eddie and the Cruisers*, was set in my home state of New Jersey. The next book, *Season for War*, would be the first of a Philippine trilogy spanning nearly 100 years of U.S. engagement with those islands.

I hadn't planned to write a book about the Philippines until my wife, a foreign correspondent for *The New York Times*, was sent there. Before that move, I hadn't focused on the century-long history that bound the U.S. and those 7,000 Pacific islands in a complicated relationship. When I was there, Ferdinand Marcos was president.

My wife lived in Manila, where the air was thick with exhaust and with smoke from burning trash and where children followed you hoping for some spare change. The city was home for millions more that it could accommodate. So, getting out was imperative. On one of those trips, a driver and guide took us to the mountains north of Manila, to an area where some of the Aeta, who are tribal descendants of the Negritos of the Andaman islands, live. They are not Filipinos. They are seldom seen. There are perhaps 25,000 people, fewer than two dozen groups, on a few Philippine Islands. Sometimes referred to as "little black persons," we had arranged to go to a village in the mountains north of Manila.

We drove past startlingly beautiful rice terraces on steep hillsides. The road was narrow, winding and rutted. Our destination was a small village with simple huts. There we were met by village elders. Our guide translated, telling my wife that our hosts probably hadn't seen a Black American woman, which was possibly why they were so fascinated by her, the children especially. One of the children suddenly dashed off, then quickly returned. In his hands was a piece of metal, about the size of a plate and wrapped in cloth. He presented it to Pamela and she unwrapped it. It was a canteen, an old canteen. It said U.S. CALVARY. The boy pointed to my wife and back to the canteen, clearly indicating some connection. The guide had no explanation.

Back in Manila, we told a friend, a bookstore owner and writer, about the trip. He speculated that the canteen had belonged to an American soldier, perhaps one of the Black soldiers, perhaps a Buffalo Soldier, possibly a deserter, who may have found a home and a family in those mountains.

And now the research began. I needed to know more about the Treaty of Paris, which in December 1898 ended the Spanish American War. For $20 million, Spain agreed to sell the Philippines to the U.S. But two days before the U.S. Congress ratified the Treaty of Paris, Filipino nationalists led by Emilio Aguinaldo clashed with American soldiers. That was the beginning of the Philippine American War. It lasted three years.

What intrigued me was the fact that among the soldiers sent to the Philippines in that war were 6,000 Black Americans, including 2,000 Buffalo Soldiers. The Buffalo Soldiers were Black men who had fought in the Indian campaigns, then in Cuba, and then were sent to the Philippines under the command of white officers. Some were in the 25th Infantry Regiment, the Black unit in my novel *Season for War*. While most of the soldiers returned to the U.S. after the war, historians believe about 30 Buffalo Soldiers deserted the U.S. Army and that more than a dozen defected to join the Filipino nationalist movement. One of the most famous defectors, David Fagen, was said to have defected to the mountain vastness of northern Luzon.

And so, I had the beginning of a story, one which required days among the archives in the basement of the New York City Public Library. The Buffalo Soldiers, who fought in the West and whose hair resembled the hide of the buffalo, thus Buffalo Soldiers, didn't leave much for the archives. In 1982, when I began my research, there were letters and some military documents. But since then, historians and documentary film makers, like Dru Holley, have expanded our knowledge of the Buffalo Soldiers. My work is fiction, but was inspired by facts and plausible events.

In the novel, one of the Buffalo Soldiers, Duquesne, sums up the challenge of the war and of his life in the Philippines.

"Yeah. Sure, lots of us hate the place. Hot weather, bad strategy, a war you couldn't find, but it dragged on forever, eight thousand miles from home, and after the first couple of battles, who gave a damn? Lost three times, four times, the men we lost in Cuba fought ten times as long and who the hell cared? But, loved it. The hot weather didn't bother me none. And, I like being in farm country. I liked the bamboo and coconuts, bananas, papayas, things I never heard of... soursops, mangosteens...But it isn't just the food. It was the feeling of the place. Evenings I'd walk out into the rice paddies, just me, and there was a thousand little ponds and terraces. Each pool would catch a piece of the sunset...It was a well-made world out there...I loved it."

ESSAYS

ESSAYS

"I'm a writer, it's what I do…"

I'd spend most of my career writing about other people, movie stars for *LIFE* magazine, business tycoons for *The Wall Street Journal*, adventurers for *National Geographic Traveler*. For many years, I was an observer, a chronicler. But I had a personal story. And in 2002 and 2003, I wrote about myself.

God the Disc Jockey, an essay published in the *Southwest Review*, a literary journal, revealed my love of 60's music and contained a confession: "What I offer in *God the Disc Jockey* is less a profession of faith than an expression of hope."

In *Breakfast in Ohio*, published in the *Antioch Review*, I confess that I'm an outsider. Yes, I'm from New Jersey, but I've lived longer in Ohio than anywhere else. When I was a runner, I ran the country roads near the college and later with a buddy we drove every inch of road in Knox County. It took years. But I am still an outsider. And when I go to breakfast, sometimes at small local restaurants with mostly trucks in the parking lot, I am aware that there are men, almost always just men, who meet informally at coffee before going to work. They enjoy a brotherhood and share private jokes. These men who meet for breakfast have one of the rarest things in the world and one of the nicest: "a cheerful table of people regularly enjoying each other's company."

In 2002, the *New England Review* published *The File Cabinet*. In the cabinet are memories and the story of my parents. There is a journal kept by my mother, which had an entry about my return home from Kenyon College for a visit. On 3/4/64 she wrote: "Fred came home around 8 p.m. with a beard. Pop is upset. Our first robin."

My Private Germany recalls the return trip my parents and I took in 1954 to Germany. That trip left me with lessons to ponder: "In Germany wars were started and lost. And, everyone with some German in them has traveled to a place no American had ever been, way out on the last frontier: defeat."

My nonfiction is often about memory, about decisions and the accidents that shaped my career. Perhaps because I visited Kenyon College on a beautiful day, it influenced my decision to apply. And when I came to Gambier, Ohio, I found a professor who invested in me and helped to shape my understanding and appreciation of literature. When he died, I was a pallbearer.

I have written extensively about Kenyon and my life in Gambier. And when I'm asked why, I answer: "I can't help feeling that I am where I ought to be."

P.F. KLUGE

WRITERS ABOUT WRITING

WRITERS ABOUT WRITING
Why You Should Learn to Write

"You may not regard writing as a career. But, it will make sense of the work you do and the life you live."

Over the years, I've taught scores of students. Very few of them become full-time writers. Some become teachers, executives, doctors, artists, lawyers, actors, entrepreneurs. For most, it took time, often lots of time, to find a successful career path. But I have discovered that regardless of what career they've chosen, they are grateful for their mastery of language and the ability to read intelligently and to compose artfully.

Among my former students is Dr. Katherine Tully, Associate Professor of Agroecology, Department of Plant Science and Landscape Architecture, the University of Maryland. She has been extraordinarily successful. I asked her why. "Because I can write," she said.

Dr. Katherine Tully

Associate Professor of Agroecology
University of Maryland

I am a scientist, but I was a writer first. My entire childhood through college, I wanted to be a novelist. I think some part of me still does. When I was young, I thought that the opposite of a writer was a scientist – someone purely analytical, bland, lacking in imagination. Someone whose nose is glued to the lab bench, and who never writes. I know differently now. All I do is write. I write grant proposals, scientific manuscripts, and presentations. I am an associate editor of two major scientific journals, shepherding others' work through the peer-review process.

The format of a scientific manuscript is prescribed and, admittedly, somewhat bland. At first, it was hard to learn how to compartmentalize my thoughts into such a rigid format. For example, you have to explain exactly what you observed in the "Results" section without giving a glimmer of why you think something occurred the way it did. *Just the facts.* Then in the "Discussion" section, you explain why you found certain changes or patterns, but without reiterating the exact finding. Most scientists loathe the "Discussion" section – my students certainly do. I love it. This is where one gets to explain, expound, conjecture, and synthesize. A good writer can weave a story into any format – haiku, sestina, or scientific manuscript. If you know what it is you want to say, you are going to figure out a way to say it.

I believe that I am good at my job because I learned early on the importance of telling a good story. Metaphors and images bring a story to life. People will listen to you if you can paint a picture for them. I believe that is why my work has been covered in *The New York Times*, *National Public Radio*, *The Atlantic*, local radio stations, and on the *TEDx* stage. The world is starving for good science communicators. Journalists ache for the biochemist who can clearly talk about the implications of gene editing in rice, the geographer who can explain the link between a shift in diets in China and the clearing of the Amazonian rainforest. However, doing science that unlocks a human mystery is not enough. You also need to know how to tell the world about it.

I learned how to be a good writer at Kenyon – but I was born loving to read and write. I am still an avid reader. Of course, I read a lot of scientific articles for work, but I try to read everything else in between – mysteries, biographies, pop science, dystopian sci-fi, poetry, westerns, family sagas, magical realism, memoirs, etc. Reading is crucial to being a good writer. It is important to be able to pause after a beautiful sentence, a perfect metaphor, an exquisite description, an exacting clip of dialogue. Maybe you can't describe why something struck you, but you recognize its power, you soak it in. Often that is enough.

I work with my graduate students to improve their ability to write. I tell my students that there is nothing more valuable in science than being a good communicator. You cannot get funded if you cannot explain why your research is important. You cannot train the next generation if you cannot break down complex topics into digestible chunks. It is important to learn how to write in different formats because not everyone is going to read your scientific article. So, you also need to break it down into a press release, a blog post, a short film, a tweet.

I have spent my life writing and I don't expect to stop. Once I lived in my imagination, creating magical lands for my characters. Now, I write about climate change – there is nothing more real and stark that I can think of. My goal is to help people understand this existential threat. To incite them to think about what they love in this world and what they are willing to do to protect it.

Rohini Pragasam
Head of Communications & Marketing
ORIX Corporation, a Tokyo-based financial
services company, New York, NY

Communications is writing. There are all kinds of associated images around the dark arts of public relations and communications, but really, at the end of the day, it is just writing. You can read those words out to a journalist, or put it in an advertisement, or spam some helpless clients via email. But whatever the delivery method, you have to be able to write.

I write for a living as a corporate communications person. I do it every single day. Sometimes it's really interesting and complex like ghost writing a CEO's heartfelt emotional response to the George Floyd killing. Sometimes it is merely procedural – "please remember to turn off your computers before you leave the office." Sometimes it's all new – how you communicate a company's culture, comfort your employees and keep everyone motivated and focused through a pandemic while thousands of you work remotely.

I write the way I think math geniuses read and interpret complex formulas. I start writing in my head, usually working out the feeling and tone of the communication. I think through the audience, what they know, what they should feel when they read the email/letter/press release. Thoughts and phrases take shape well before I sit down to "put pen to paper." When I do sit, I write all at once, with the various word combinations and turns of phrases spilling out. One thing I have learned along the way is not to be afraid of moving things around. I used to be very terrified of changing the order of things as they made their way from my brain to the document. Now I think the best work comes from moving things around a lot, like a seating chart for a wedding, to see what works best and what makes sense.

I also have learned to live graciously with the redline edit. In my profession I don't have the luxury of sending my writing out directly into the universe. It usually goes through management types, lawyers – inside and outside – colleagues and sometimes a place called Compliance that operates as a disclaimer dispensing center. I used to take the redline edits very personally and argue each one with the people asking for changes. I have learned now that, as with the rest of life, you can have too much pride. Not everyone writes in the same way, and that can be either cause for frustration or what makes things interesting.

When people cannot write it does drive me crazy. I don't mind if bankers or IT folks can't write – it's not their center of expertise. When communications people cannot write it boggles the mind. I do try and write by example and hope some of it sinks in with the people whose work I am reviewing and editing. Nothing makes me happier than improvement and seeing thoughtfulness and attention to detail.

I am forever grateful to those who patiently, or not so patiently, showed me the way through a story's arc, helped me to understand the power of structure and perhaps the most difficult part – how to stop when you are done.

Megan Wolpert Dobkin
Producer of film/TV/music videos
Big Kid Pictures, Los Angeles, CA

It took me fifteen years working closely with writers to finally admit I was one. I was never shy about my love of storytelling: fiction, theater, film – but the story I had told myself was that I was best suited as a doula at the birth of other writers' babies, cheerleading and coaching in the Hollywood studio system as a script development executive and eventually a producer.

Every long-term project I ever personally wrote started with a panic attack and a journal entry.

When I burnt out of that Hollywood job and needed a spiritual walk-about, I took a writing class. I am not a panic attack-y kind of gal, but the structural changes I was making in my life plus the upheaval of personal writing exercises brought a lot up to the surface I didn't know I had. Darkness. Complexities. Sadness. Internal contradictions. Flags you can't really fly while holding productions together on set. My partner and I were building a house together when I stepped back from my career. I was a lava lamp and futon chick when we met, domesticity and choosing faucets was not my forte. I was on a research mission to find doorstop options when I had my first panic attack. I was curious where it was coming from, so I journaled about it. Picked at its wound. I wanted to know more. What was this extreme reaction I was having to domesticity? Was it actually mine? Or inherited from a different generation?

I spent the next six months rolling around in these questions – taking classes on cooking, flower arranging, scrapbooking, quilting – anything that scared the shit out of me and I journaled through it. What I discovered about myself was both profound and a little scary. It became my first attempt at a book. My second panic attack occurred at the breast-feeding seminar I took when I was pregnant with my first child. Like – had to leave, put my head between my knees and breathe through a paper bag kind of leave.

Answering the question of why that happened became my second book. There are many kinds of writers in the world – who use writing for many different reasons. I guess I am the kind that uses it to discover and lay bare personal secrets I don't normally communicate in the absence of writing. I am most brave when I write. I am most healed when I dig deep and get cozy with my Ugly. And, in order to do that, I usually have to take my marketing/executive hat off – the one that is asking "who is this story for" until the piece itself tells me. The answer has, many times in the past, been "for no one." If I hadn't returned to my producing job with a new, more sustainable way of doing it – and I was relying on this writing to provide for me and my family, this would present a problem. Such is the great tragedy of the art and commerce intersection. And also an endorsement for not thinking of the healing art of writing only as a career.

Process wise, I am deeply grateful that I picked up the pen for the first-time during motherhood. I can write anywhere – with anything happening around me because I didn't have a decade of developing ritual around my writing. I know many writers who can only write in a certain place, with a certain amount of time and noise level. I learned to write during 45-minute naps. I know that if I am graced with four hours, I can dip into a project that is more in its initial creation phase – something that is in more need of space around me. If I have a 30-minute stretch, that is usable time for re-reading, for editing, for that smaller piece. In fact, while I had young babies and toddlers, I had a boom of published flash fiction and poetry for exactly that reason. All time is usable. Even a drive in the car is fruitful if I am asking myself a specific enough question to crack. Having boundaries around checking email or social media before writing is beyond necessary. At best those things engage the executive functioning (not fluid and intuitive) side of the brain. At worst it steals valuable life force you will need to exert excess labor to get back. I am also a believer in a good Sunday night scheduling session to spot writing opportunities during the week. Do everything in your power to protect them. If you can't, find another spot to make up that time.

And score yourself a good pair of noise cancellation headphones which should be used to silence the internal noise – the expectation of what a writing practice and career "should" look like – as much as that loud cafe.

WRITERS ABOUT WRITING
My Professional Journey

"A writer's luggage comprises memories,
which writing turns into keepers."

The Journalist: My first paid job was as a reporter at the *Wall Street Journal* in Los Angeles. I wrote mostly features, stories that were more entertaining than financial. By contrast, my wife really was a financial writer, first for the *Wall Street Journal* and then for *The New York Times*. When I met her, she was a summer intern at the *Wall Street Journal* in Los Angeles, her second internship before graduate school. She would become a financial reporter in Philadelphia and New York City for the *WSJ*, specializing in corporate profiles and industry trends. Years later she taught economics and business journalism at Columbia University's graduate school of journalism and edited a text for financial journalists. By contrast, at the *Wall Street Journal*, I wrote mostly non-financial stories: *California Town Lives with Sonic Boom, The Then Generation: Lawrence Welk*, which was reprinted in *Catholic Digest*. Then, there were my decline stories: *Bygone Battles: American Legion...A Time of Change* and *Closing Time: Neighborhood Bars in America*. Perhaps I was more of an entertainment writer, at least *LIFE* magazine thought so. From the *Wall Street Journal* in Los Angeles., I moved to NYC and to *LIFE*, where my assignments included profiles of John Wayne and Ann-Margaret.

The Screen Writer: When I wrote *Eddie and the Cruisers*, I didn't have a film in mind. I got lucky, at least at the start, when I was approached by a filmmaker who optioned the novel. During the shooting and editing of the film, I made small contributions. The film was only "inspired" by my book. When the film was released and shown in movie theaters, I was not inspired. While *Eddie* would eventually become a cult classic, in 1983, when it was released, it earned only $4 million in theaters. But then in 1984 *Eddie and the Cruisers* was shown on HBO. That marketing move, according to Geoff Edgars, a writer for *The Washington Post*, started the cable revolution. And when videocassette recorders were becoming popular, *Eddie* became even more successful and the music more popular. "The VCR turned movie songs into hit songs," observed the writer Sherman Alexie, who wrote the forward to a paperback edition of *Eddie*. In my home office I have a gold record and a platinum record that celebrate the sale of millions of records of the soundtrack.

I don't love the film, but there are moments that I'm proud of. In one scene Ellen Barkin, playing a reporter, urges Tom Berenger, the Cruiser's "Wordman," to answer questions about Eddie. He hesitates. Then his reply, which comes directly from the novel: "I knew him a long time. And you, I just met."

The Constitution Writer: I was back on my Peace Corps islands in Micronesia in 1975, hired this time to serve as a director of the Constitutional Convention that would end the last of the United Nations' trust territories. The Trust Territory of the Pacific Islands was to become the Federated States of Micronesia. The constitution needed a Preamble. I sat down and wrote it:

*We, the People of Micronesia, exercising our inher-
ent sovereignty, do hereby establish this Constitution
of the Federated States of Micronesia.*

*With this Constitution, we affirm our common wish
to live together in peace and harmony, to preserve the
heritage of the past, and to protect the promise of
the future.*

*To make one nation of many islands, we respect the
diversity of our cultures. Our differences enrich us.
The seas bring us together, they do not separate us.
Our islands sustain us, our island nation enlarges us
and makes us stronger.*

*Our ancestors, who made their homes on these
islands, displaced no other people. We, who remain,
wish no other home than this. Having known war,
we hope for peace. Having been divided, we wish
unity. Having been ruled, we seek freedom.*

*Micronesia began in the days when man explored
seas in rafts and canoes. The Micronesian nation is
born in an age when men voyage among the stars; our
world itself is an island. We extend to all nations
what we see from each: peace, friendship, coopera-
tion, and love in our common humanity. With this
Constitution we, who have been the ward of other
nations, become the proud guardian of our own
islands, now and forever.*

I had not expected to become this kind of writer. When
asked why a writer, not a lawyer, should write the preamble, my short answer is: "A constitution is a work of

fiction." It expresses, I contend, a country's aspirations and a hoped-for reality.

The Speech Writer: I was a speech writer briefly. While living in New York City, calls would come in the middle of the night, usually from across the planet and from a tiny Pacific island group, called The Republic of Palau. In the 1980s, the President of the Republic of Palau, Lazarus Salii often needed my help, especially when he was invited to the United Nations where he was expected to address the assembly. He would come to town for a few days. We'd consult and I'd write a speech that he'd deliver. And, if there was time, I'd invite him to get to know my island of Manhattan as he'd welcomed me to get to know his.

These days, I give the speeches. And here's a tip for writers: While bookstores may seem the obvious place to talk about your books and your work, it is often better to address a captive audience – people who, for various reasons, must attend your talk. For example, on Semester at Sea, a floating university that usually carries about 800 students, I gave a lecture titled: "How Novels Are Born." To a workshop at the University of Akron, I asked, and answered, the question: "Can Writing Be Taught?" To the Association of College Counselors in Independent Schools in San Francisco, I tackled the topic: "A Recommendation Regarding Recommendations." I was not always talking about my books, but every introduction made it clear that I was a writer.

The Education Writer: Several years ago, I gave an address to the Council of Colleges of Arts and Sciences annual meeting. I was invited because of *Alma Mater*, which is a month-by-month nonfiction account of a year in the life of a liberal arts college, Kenyon College, my alma mater. My address was controversial, tough love, but still a loving, account of a year in the life of a liberal arts college. The San Francisco appearance not only helped sales of the book, but it encouraged debate. It was exposure for me and publicity for the book, which was further aided by a reprint of the speech in a special section of the *Chronicle of Higher Education*, which reaches thousands of educators.

The Writer-in-Residence: I teach. I give lectures and speeches. I write. And the result of this activity and the writing it produces, could be called "The Portable Kluge," except that that sounds too much like an urn full of ashes, sometimes known as "cremains." Instead, the collection is called *Keepers*. And, according to my wife, it reveals more of me than anything I've written. It begins on page three with a credo: "If you're a writer, nothing is ever over until it's written down…A writer's luggage comprises memories, which writing turns into keepers."

The position, Writer-in-Residence, does not exist at most colleges and universities. And, if it does, it's usually a short-term arrangement for a well-known or promising writer who's finished a manuscript. As a visitor, the writer-in-residence might do some teaching or conduct seminars. What made me different was that I was not passing through. I was a member of the faculty for 25 years. And as a faculty member, I was subject to occasional performance reviews. For one of these Faculty Performance Reviews, the editor of the highly-regarded *Kenyon Review* was an evaluator. It was a letter that nicely summed up my contribution to the college:

"I have read a great deal of Fred Kluge's writing, both fiction and nonfiction. His work is of a very high caliber indeed. I am amazed that he is so disciplined as to write productively even while teaching multiple classes. He is, in many ways, an ideal "writer-in-residence." Were I forced to choose, I would confess that I prefer Professor Kluge's nonfiction writing. He is a born journalist, able to bring to bear all his powers of observation and consideration. A perfect example is the essay *My Private Germany* which I published recently in *The Kenyon Review*. It is a beautiful piece of work."

– David H. Lynn,
Editor, *The Kenyon Review*, Oct 12, 2009

THE CLASSROOM

CAN WRITING BE TAUGHT?

"Writing is a matter of seeing before saying."

C an writing be taught? That's a tricky question. Should writing be taught? I can imagine "no" answers to these questions. Shouldn't students spend their time reading great novels, short stories, essays, instead of wrestling with first paragraphs? Talented and committed as my writing students might be, they might not be ready to contend with student reviews of their work in addition to a professor-critic presiding over the criticism. How cruel and discouraging might that be, pain and a sense of failure and resentment that might last for years.

"I can't teach you to write," I announce in the first minutes of their first class. "But I can talk to you about the writing you do. The impulse to write, the sense that writing is an imperative, has to come from you," I say. "I can't have the ideas for your story. You have to see the story. Writing is much a matter of seeing...before saying."

A writing seminar, I add, is unlike any other course. Usually, students read (or skim) what the professor assigns, write papers, endure pop quizzes, confront a final exam. Conventional class, conventional results. Respectable.

From the start, students in my seminars competed to get into the course by submitting writing samples. In recent years, the first students to register for the course, get in. I'd expected that there might be a difference, that the first-come-first-serve approach to class registration would not yield as satisfying a result as the competitive approach. But I was wrong.

My classes were limited to a dozen, though at times, I've accepted one or two more. And, it is a seminar requiring students to read and discuss each other's work. Each week half the students have work under discussion. I am ruthless about attendance. "You cannot prosper in a class you do not attend."

So in each semester, I confront a dozen students sitting around a seminar table. At the first class, I congratulate the group for taking a risk with their talent, a risk to their ego. My welcome is heartfelt, mixing encouragement with the very real challenge that getting work published is difficult. Failure is real, I say.

I'm not, I warn, looking for beautiful writing or self-serving displays of sensitivity and vocabulary. "I want a story," I say. At the end, quoting writer Alice McDermott, I tell them that their work must survive one question: "So what?"

THE WRITING SEMINAR

"Plot is not a story."

In my opening seminar, I tell students that the course will be unlike any other fiction writing seminar they've ever had or will have. It operates with singular intensity, a sense of talent revealing itself and being tested. Other classes respond, pretty straightforwardly, to effort; the harder you work, the better you do. When talent is on the table, the rules change. When students believe themselves to be talented – or at least hope they are – the stakes are higher. And I walk a line between encouraging talent, generously, and cautioning my students that they are embarked upon one of the more difficult enterprises on the planet, where the odds against commercial and/or artistic success can be daunting. You never have it made.

So it begins. Every seminar is different, as different as the complement of passengers on a ship, from voyage to voyage. Yet some things are constant. We begin with exercises on dialogue and sense of place. These are pump-priming exercises, emphasizing important elements of storytelling. Then we move into stories, which arrive in three installments. (Typically, half the seminar has work under scrutiny, every week.) All work is circulated in advance, commented upon in writing and around the seminar table. This includes weekly typed-out evaluations from me. The most important thing is to get students to talk honestly, critically, helpfully, about each other's work. I try to help students find their way without minimizing the challenges of accomplishing good work. Writing is hard, I tell them. It is also imperative.

Introduction to Fiction Writing, as I teach it, includes reading. I require just one text, Tobias Wolff's *Vintage Book of American Short Stories*. We read one story each week. It's a writer's reading, concentrating as much on *how* a story works as *what* it says; on matters of voice, tense, pace, chronology, on all the authorial decisions that make a story turn out the way it has, all the fictional strategies that involve costs and benefits. We read Raymond Carver's *Cathedral* to discover how little needs to happen in a story and Stuart Dybek's *Chopin in Winter* to discover how much, how many themes, a story can contain. We read conventionally structured stories like Carol Bly's poignant *Talk of the Heroes* and we read rule-breakers like Tim O'Brien's *The Things They Carried*. It's important to do this, to sometimes turn away from a table full of starts and stops, fragments and experiments, to confront finished, accomplished work. It's as important as the writing. They're inseparable. Reading is the inhale, writing is the exhale. Without both, you cannot breathe.

I ask myself what I've accomplished in all these years of seminars. These are students who, after all, could be taking Shakespeare and Milton. I've produced some published writers, some journalists, some publishers, editors, agents and many, very many, alert and critical readers. The seminar isn't about turning out professional writers, though I'm all for it. It's about developing an engagement with language and story. It's about clarity, coherence, sometime elegance. About making connections in life. Also, about a life-long distaste for circumlocution, verbosity, evasion: a built-in "bullshit detector." Most of all it's about evaluating life, one's own life and the lives of others.

A first class goes like this: "You didn't have to take this course." I tell them. "I'm glad you did. And I hope you'll feel the same. But now I want to talk about the story you'll write, submitting ten-page installments, every other week. I calculate you'll be turning in fifty to sixty pages. That doesn't amount to cruel and unusual punishment."

I pause. These students couldn't know how much I like them. Maybe they could guess.

"BUT," I continue, "there will be cruel and punishing moments, now and then, maybe – obviously – on your first drafts, possibly on your final. I'll say it again. I can't teach you how to write. But I can talk to you about the writing you do. And everyone else will be doing the same thing. You can write down their comments, which can be all over the place. Contradictory. Go faster, go slower, more of this, less of that. What's funny or isn't funny, what's supposed to be scary or was predictable. There's no way you can accommodate all of these complaints. Don't even try. Sort through and decide what works."

They will write a story, with a cast of characters, impending crisis or conflict and some sort of resolution, happy or sad. "But writing a story is not the same as devising a plot. A story is about complicated mixed human beings. A plot is a string of gimmicks. Plot is not story. Think about human experience and situations. The plot is the last thing to think about. In fact, you shouldn't think about it at all."

"How do you start a story?" This is from one of the busy note takers.

"You think about it first," I say. "The thinking that you do before you write word one is crucial. You don't just start cranking out words, hoping that a story shows up. Where is the story set? And when? Who are your characters, major and minor? What's the conflict at the heart of the story? What's the ending, the mood and meaning?"

"That's what we have to know. That's what you need to discover," I say. This is their – and my – introduction to writing. From early stuff – diaries and letters and home-work to journalism, to writing – and in my case, teaching writing. We're all in the same boat: writing. I'm at the helm. They're working the oars.

Some students sail along, trusting their talent. Look ma, no hands! Excellent! The others will learn about criticism, revisions. A mixed group. Some students, initially average, will surge. Some will face disappointments, some pleas-ing surprises. And sometime there'd be a student who just doesn't belong. I think of them as "sucking chest wounds." But there is always a chance they'd be sharp readers, one of a handful of students who earn immediate attention when they raise their hands.

I sit there, musing about the hundred or more students I've taught. Some – half a dozen maybe – are well-known professionals whose two or three best sellers far exceed-ed my own works. Some were acclaimed right out of the gate. They'd be stars at their fifth reunion, if they came. They are generous, on line, in crediting me with help, wis-dom, occasional drinks on the porch in back of my house.

Others will be published much later. It takes time for the returns to come in.

I don't exactly say, but I indicate my respect for the students who take my seminar. Most college courses are honorably and predictably straightforward. If you did a bit of everything, adequately, you are a B student. B-minus is a warning. And a C means "average." That is a downer. Our one-block college town is a congenial spot. But when you cross paths with a C-student, what happens? I'd been quoted on this point, in a way that the college provost – or dean of students – would not be pleased. "It's like you're crossing paths with a student who you last saw when you were in the waiting room of a venereal clinic."

EVALUATIONS

"Despite his faults, he is the best kind of Kenyon professor"
– A student critique

These days, I make use of an office, attached to my garage and, thus, my home. It's a cluttered place and I am amazed by the things that I find. It's as if they've been waiting for me. I find two reports from former provost Gregory Spaid. These are student evaluations of my performance as a professor. Instantly, I am riveted.

The first is dated 2003. "He is a piece of Kenyon and of Gambier, a near icon in the classroom whom students find "engaging," "clever," "funny," energetic," "sharp," and – beware of what comes next – "intimidating." That word crops up again and again. One student showed mercy. "Sometimes it's hard to break the surface of him and he can be intimidating due to his arrogance." But, she adds, she had "nothing but a good experience" with me.

"There was an almost universal sense among...students that your comments on their work are helpful, timely, and generous. They praise you for your genuine interest in them and their work and for your willingness to meet them at almost any time or place," the provost says.

Now, 2008. "One student calls you a prick," reports the provost, "which is the first time such earthly candor appears in a faculty review." But, the provost acknowledges that an overwhelming majority of students support me.

One says: "His criticism was never cruel as such, because it was passionate. He was angry when students turned in stories that hadn't been proofread, stories awash in grammatical errors and incomplete thoughts. This honest feedback helped to develop my own critical eye, which I think is the most important tool a writer can have." From another student: "He spoke and wrote and humored his way through difficult criticism of our work. I loved it and I feared it. This was when I began to think of myself as a writer." And a final paragraph. "In summary I want to make clear that I cannot be more effusive in my feedback on Professor Kluge. He will remain an inseparable part of everything I remember as distinctly, positively Kenyon. Despite his faults, he is the best kind of Kenyon professor, one whose guidance outside of the classroom is as valuable and possibly more resonant than his lectures. Kenyon owes him a raise. And a drink."

SERIOUS BUSINESS

"Struggling with a story that makes
what matters to us matter to others..."

L et me be clear. I don't believe that writing classes require published authors. Dedicated readers might be as – or more – discerning than I can be. Still, unfair as it may be, there's no denying that a class will be impressed if their teacher has published a stack of books. Those students and I have something in common: struggling with a story that makes what matters to us matter to others. We're all in the same boat. It won't be long before I tell them what we share and what we don't.

What's interesting about a writing class is that, in addition to attempting to impress me, students are trying to impress each other. They're competing. A history or a chemistry class goes about its normal business. This is different. It's competitive and it's personal.

I tell them, "I'm not going to sit here and say 'begin a story…the first eight pages say – and e-mail it to everyone next Friday.' "That's not how it works," I say. "Most of the class, you'll be going over each other's stories. These are fragmentary first drafts. I wouldn't like, you wouldn't like it if we spent two hours vivisecting your stories. We'd all go a little crazy." I pause before adding "I'd be out of my mind, altogether."

Some students got it. Others I wasn't sure of. They weren't sure either.

When I was done, I scanned the table. When you stand at a podium, you're dominant. Not so around a table. I saw assiduous note takers, doodlers, careful listeners and two or three who looked stunned and oblivious.

"Any questions? We've been here two hours. We're done. But you can drop by my office any time. I get lonely there."

BLAST FROM THE PAST

Dear Fred,

Greetings from a ghost of Kenyon Past! I'm hoping you may remember your first Fiction Writing Seminar at Kenyon, c. 1988, of which I was a proud member. I remember there was quite a lot of buzz in the lead up to your arrival on campus. First off, the English Department didn't offer any fiction writing courses in those days. Secondly, word on the Path was that you were Mr. Lentz's mysterious, commercially successful doppelganger, come back to rattle his cage. In any case, I had publishing aspirations myself, and made damn sure I got into that seminar.

I have great memories of our Wednesday night classes that fall – settling into the circle of chairs with a dozen students, girding up for some good old-fashioned, cripplingly constructive criticism. My friend Charlie was also in the class, and we used to stop at the deli and bring a Fosters Lager to sip over the two hours. I'm not sure it was legal, but it felt very Hemingway. For one assignment, tapping into the creepy-beautiful vibe Gambier offers in October, I wrote a ghost story of twenty pages, composed almost entirely at night in Sunset Cottage. You stumbled upon me there once. I think I startled you. "A college kid writing on a Friday night for fun in a dark cottage?" you said. "You may have what it takes." This was fairly close to a compliment, I reasoned, and I decided I'd take it.

Well, I'm writing to let you know my first novel, *The Stepping Off Place*, releases next May from HarperCollins. It took…well, it took some time, but it's happening at last. And you fit into my road to publication in a couple of ways. I've been meaning to write you to tell you how it sold – at auction in a two-book deal! – last September.

After Kenyon, I went into teaching (you wrote my recommendation for graduate school), married, started a family, and finally got back to writing fiction in the mid 00s. I joined a critique group and got serious about publishing, and over several years, I wrote two middle-grade novels (for ages 8-12) that could never quite sell. Then, John Green's *The Fault in Our Stars* came out to all its acclaim, and I snapped it up, excited Kenyon had produced yet another literary superstar. I was blown away. The writing was so accessible and beautiful, funny and weirdly familiar to me. In more than one interview I listened to, John Green refer to you and your mentorship. Exhilarated by the one – one! – degree of separation between me and a young adult phenom, I decided to try my hand at YA. I'd lost my best teenage friend around the same time, and the genre allowed me to process my grief. That's where *The Stepping Off Place* came from, and it landed me a senior agent at Writers House and eventually the two-book deal with HarperCollins. So, thank you for inspiring me, and also for inspiring John Green, who then, however unwittingly, inspired me as well. You are the kind of teacher that students don't forget, and I'm so happy I fought my way into that seminar in 1988.

I hope life has treated you magnificently since then. I would love to catch up via a phone call. Please let me know if you'd be game for that.

All my best,
Cameron R. '89

PS – My husband, also an educator, became a fan of yours when he read *Alma Mater*. We bought it on one of our two visits to Kenyon, and he read it in a single sitting. He loaned it to a fellow educator and never got it back, a fact which provokes much muttering and creative swearing to this day. I must remedy that.

"YOUR OLD STUDENT MAKES GOOD"
John Green

Date: Tuesday, February 25, 2003 7:17 PM
From: John Green
To: P.F. Kluge
Subject: your old student makes good

Kluge, I know you're traveling, but I'm hoping you're checking your email. Ever since sophomore year of college, there's been one burning question in my life: Who was right?

Was Kluge right? Did I have some (admittedly unharnessed) talent for writing? Was there a chance that the perennial virgin, desperate for every sort of love, might one day become a real, honest-to-goodness author?

Or was David Lynn right to reject me for the Advanced Fiction Writing class – to dismiss me out of hand, as a wanna-be who never would be?

Well, Dutton just agreed to publish my first novel, a YA novel about three kids at a boarding school in Alabama (Professor Lentz might recognize the setting as his alma mater).

So, you were right after all. Thanks for your encouragement. You taught me pretty much everything I know about writing stories. And you also kept me writing. I was devastated when I didn't get into the advanced class. I don't know if I would have kept writing if you hadn't been kind to me.

David Shargel forwarded me your article from *The Chronicle of Higher Education*, which was a wonderful piece of writing. I agree with everything you said, but know this: for all the Kamp Kenyoness of the place (and God knows I Kamped with the best of them), you're the closest thing to a Denham Sutcliffe, an "eloquent sardonic" man who made us take off our hats and take this shit seriously.

Thanks, John Green

Note: John Green, the author of *The Fault in Our Stars*, *Looking for Alaska* and *Paper Towns*, has sold more than 50 million books worldwide.

AFTER THOUGHTS

...an aunt presented me with my handwritten account of my first sea voyage to Europe. She'd tied together the pages with a white satin ribbon.

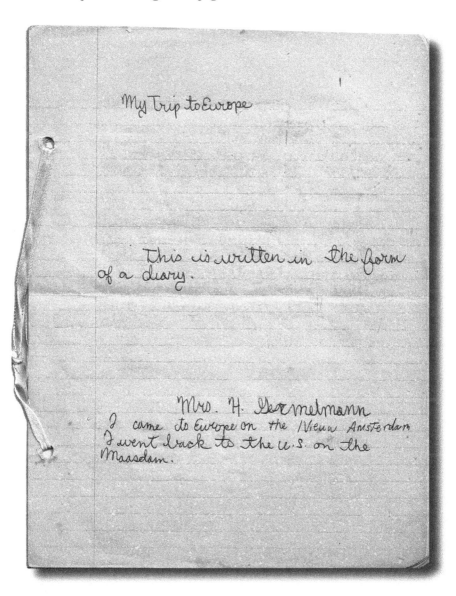

My Trip to Europe

This is written in the form of a diary.

Mrs. H. Germelmann

I came to Europe on the Nieuw Amsterdam
I went back to the U.S. on the Maasdam.

WHEN I WAS TWELVE
My Trip to Europe, May 1954

The following is my first piece of reporting. It was travel writing and journalism. Was I a budding writer at 12-years old?

Getting a Vaccination

One night Father and I went to Dr. Hohenstein to get a vaccination. Mom had already gotten her vaccination from Dr. Peters. The law says you have to get a vaccination if you plan to travel in a foreign country. At that time it did not hurt at all. But about 3 days after getting the vaccination my arm got sore and swollen, but 2 days later that was all gone.

I came to Europe on the Nieuw Amsterdam. I went back to the U.S. on the Maasdam.

May 21, Friday

I woke up rather early and got out of bed at 7:30. At 9:00 Jimmy came to pick us up. It was raining outside. At a little before 10:00 we were in Hoboken. We saw the ship with some of the relatives that had to stay behind. Then we said good bye to everyone and the ship set sail. Boy, oh Boy, this sure is a wonderful boat. It has movies, stores and wonderful restaurants. We are about 3-5 miles out at sea now and as I write I look outside the window I can see the sea sweeping by. The rain stopped a little before we went on the boat but the sun is not out and it is windy and rather cold. (THE PREVIOUS PART WAS WRITTEN AT 2:00. NOW I WRITE IN BED). At 4:30 I went to the movies and saw *Quo Vadis*. It was very good. I am not yet sea sick. It still seems hard to believe that we are on a big ocean liner headed toward Europe. At 4:00 o'clock we had a fire drill. It is rather easy to put on a life preserver but I do not think I would like to go swimming in that ocean outside. I wonder how my schoolmates in Columbia School are doing. I will have to write them a postcard or letter from Rotterdam. The crew is friendly, and they speak English fluently even though most of them are Dutch. The boat is spotlessly clean.

May 22, Saturday

Tonight after spending my first night at sea I was still healthy as could be. Uncle Fritz and Aunt Carie got seasick. Uncle Fritz recovered very quickly. Aunt Carie is just so-so. The ocean is just about the same as it was yesterday. Today I got an edition of the ship's newspaper. I went to the movies today and saw *All I Desire*. It was very good. The meals are excellent. Every afternoon they serve tea and cookies. I have the cookies but I don't drink tea. Tante Helen, even though she is traveling cabin class, eats with us in the tourist class restaurant. There is also a little bit of gambling on board the ship. They race little wooden horses around a little race track painted on canvas. If when they roll 2 big dice on the floor one number is

6, that is the number of the horse that moves, and the other dice shows how many jumps the horse takes. 25¢ a chance. They also race live turtles and play Bingo, keno and lotto. The cabin steward gives me stamps off letters that people get. He is very nice. So is most everybody on board for that matter. I sleep in the upper berth of our little room. I would not trade it for anything.

May 23, Sunday

Today we missed church services. All the food was very good today. Last night we saw an iceberg. We were eating supper when the public address system announced that an iceberg could be seen from the portside. For the first 5 minutes we could not see anything, and many people thought that it was a big joke, but then we saw a large iceberg about 3 miles or more away. There were still a few rays of sunlight which shone over the water, and the scene was quite beautiful. Many people let their imaginations get the best of them and they imagined that the iceberg was a strange sort of ship, which it certainly was not. As we passed the iceberg it seems to turn black. That was be- cause sunlight was not hitting it in that direction. We must remember that only 1/10 of an iceberg is above water and that 9/10 of it is below water. I went to the movies with Pop and Uncle Fritz and saw *Escape from Fort Bravo*. It was very good.

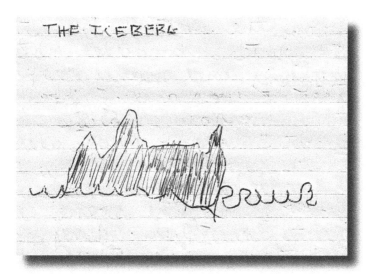

May 24, Monday

Today we were told about the different types of
Badges. It was really quite interesting.

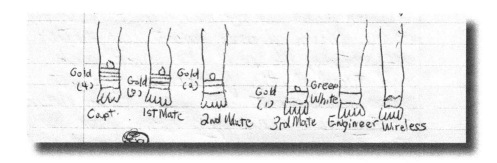

I played shuffleboard and ping pong today. I also went
to the movies and saw *The Pony Express*, it was very good.
Today they had horse races and live turtle races. But I did
not risk any money by betting. I lost 75¢ the other day
on Bingo and that was enough. Willy told me that all the
stewards sleep in the front of the ship. There are usually
about 6 in one room. Today we had a tour of the ship, it
was mostly through first class. They have a neat gymnasi-
um. I was told that last night a man came down from first
class, rather disgusted, he said he was sick and tired of
the fanciness of first class and that he had come down to
tourist class for some fun. He treated everyone to a beer
and had a good time. I am having a lot fun on board ship.
I copied this from a map on the wall.

DATE	RUN	WIND	SEA	SWELL
M-22	469	SSW/2	Ripple	Low
M.23	423	SSE3	Smooth	Low
M-24	494	N3	Smooth	Low
M-25	484	NW6	Rough	Moderate

Our ship has two smokestacks.

ORANGE
GREEN
WHITE
Green
ORANGE

OUR SMOKESTACK

N.A.S.M. stands for Nederlandsch Amerikaansche Stoomvaart Maatschappij. I also learned that at this time the Nieuw Amsterdam is 16 years old, and it was built in Rotterdam. It was used as a troop transport during the war. It was later remodeled. Its captain is C. Visser. It weighs more than 36,000 tons. I saw the captain and several other high ranking officers today. Tonight we are halfway.

May 25, Tuesday

Today when I woke up we found a rather rough sea. Few people had slept well during the night, and many were seasick because we had run into a baby storm just like I had wished for and had predicted. I had the Asst. Chief Steward and the table steward sign this book today. I will try and get Willy to sign it tomorrow. There are a lot of nice kids aboard. I did not play shuffleboard and ping pong today but I did play 3 games of checkers. When we arrive in Europe it is Mom and Pop's wedding anniversary. I saw *Kiss Me Kate* last night. It was very good. I spent most of my time in the library today.

May 26, Wednesday

Today we did not see any fishing boats but tomorrow we will see both fishing boats and land. We will see land late in the afternoon. At night we will be able to see the port lights. The day after tomorrow we will dock in Southampton early in the morning. Tomorrow I will try and get the captain's autograph for my diary. Pop will give me 50¢ if I can do it. Today like yesterday I spent a large amount of my time in the library. Today it was rather nice outside. They had the farewell dinner tonight. It was very nice. I played checkers, ping pong and deck shuffleboard today. I also got Willy to sign my diary. I will really hate to leave this boat. I will miss Willy and Johnny and everybody. I will also miss the food. Today they played Bingo. I was given 75¢ to gamble but I only used 25¢ of it. I shall save the rest.

May 27, Thursday

Today was a very big day. While I was at a children's party in first class, I spotted the first fishing boats. A little after lunchtime we spotted the first land, the Scilly Islands, which are in the English Channel, and several lighthouses. The first couple of islands were barren and rocky, but the larger ones were inhabited. One man told me that the people farm here and they produce most of the flour used by England. At about 3 we spotted England and have been seeing it on and off ever since then. There also are a great amount of ships in the channel. There are many fishing boats in the channel. I have heard that Holland's herring fleet went out yesterday. It seems that whatever boat catches the first herring races back to Holland and wins a prize. For the first few weeks the herrings are very expensive and cost about 30 or 40 Dutch cents. But then all of a sudden they go down to about 15-10 cents.

About 50 seagulls have been following the boat all day. Tomorrow very early we dock in Southampton. I am going to get up very early and see the proceedings. Today I got the captain's autograph for my diary. I also saw all the instruments used in controlling the ship. I also got many other autographs yesterday. We have been near the places where the Flying Enterprise with Capt. Karlson sunk and where the liner Lusitania sank from World War I. The sea was calm today. The weather was good and bad, mostly bad.

May 28, Freitag

Today was a big day. I was up at about 4:30 and out on deck at 5:00 to watch them dock in Southampton. The first thing that I noticed were the large oil refineries in Southampton. Even though it was rather early there were many other ships in the harbor. Then as we moved out of the harbor at about 8:00 I noticed 2 water forts in which they put anti-aircraft guns in time of war. I also saw some aircraft carriers. On the one that was very close to us I saw a helicopter. I imagine that the one far away had one also. We clocked in Le Havre at 3:00 in the afternoon. It was a modern city but I noticed quite a bit of rubble. Up a little was a large hill. There it looked quite pleasant. I noticed 2 churches and many other important looking buildings on top of the hill. Tomorrow at about 4:00 we are in the hook. Then when the pilot comes we start into the hook towards Rotterdam. At 5:30 or 5:00 I want to be up on deck.

May 29, Samstag

Today it was still dark and raining when we went into the hook. We found Von Wolsen without too much trouble. They had been waiting for the boat to dock, only on the wrong side of the harbor. We thought we might go straight to Stuttgart by train right away because it was raining. I can hardly believe that Rotterdam only a few years ago was a mass of rubble. Everything seems to be brand new. In the afternoon I went with Hans to see the Hague. It sure is a beautiful and wonderful building. It seems that nearly every country chipped in and contributed something to the building of it. There are beautiful trees and flowers and little ponds all over. It is still used. Two times a year the ambassadors from every foreign country that still belongs to that council gather together there and discuss the financial problems. After seeing the Hague, Hans and I walked down to the Nordsee. I was very much surprised to see a little boy about 7 years old smoking a cigarette. I also saw a man scooping up shells with a kind of a net. I did not see any dikes or wooden shoes. The only wooden shoes that I saw were the ones on the tourist stands. In front of every house is a rather large ditch filled with water. They are used to drain the property. The soil that I saw was black as black could be. I saw several wind mills. I also saw helicopters which seat 8 persons flying around the city.

May 30, Sonntag

Early in the morning we had breakfast shortly after we woke up. We took a taxi to the railroad station which was not too far away. Mr. Van Wolson was at the station to bid us farewell. He gave Onkel Fritz and I some stamps. After a short wait we hopped onto the Rheingold express which headed in the direction of Deutschland.

We saw several wind mills and cathedrals. The train was first examined by the Dutch Police and then after we got over the German border the German Police examined it. I like the way the German Police said "Guten Morgen." I have seen much livestock especially horses and cows. Soon we shall be over the German frontier. Shortly after entering Germany we went through many large towns. There is much rubble but there are also very many new buildings. The Rhine is beautiful. There are many long flat river barges on it from many different countries. I saw barges from Switzerland, Holland, and of course Germany. Occasionally I could see one of the old side wheelers like we used to have on the Mississippi River. There seem to be cattle on every hill, and believe me there sure are a lot of hills. We saw the Niederwalddenkmal, it looks just like the Statue of Liberty. It is a famous monument which commemorates a famous battle. We also saw the famous Lorelei Rock. A tunnel has been built through it in recent years and there is also a road around it. We did not have an opportunity to eat.

We all said that we would not cry when we arrived in Stuttgart. Well there is where we made a mistake. We all cried except Pop as far as I could see. Most everybody I had ever heard of in letters was there and there were still some left over. I have never seen so much pure joy before and probably never will again. After that we went to a hall where all of us could be together for a while. I got a model ship from Tante Marta and the toy shop owner in Winnenden. It was very nice. I really like everyone. We slept at Onkel Walter's. When we were in Rotterdam, Tante Helen threw up from sea sickness even though she was no longer at sea.

Dear Tante Helen,
Better tie this together.

DECADES LATER

I am at sea again. I write this on a ship anchored in Valparaiso, Chile at the end of a sea voyage that began in Buenos Aires over two weeks ago. This seems a fitting close to decades of travel, some of it by sea. That 12-year-old had no idea what he'd become or that over the years he'd travel and write and somehow make a living doing it.

MY FATHER COMES TO AMERICA, 1923

*"I was the first one to cross the ocean and start a new life over here.
Let me try to tell you all about it." — Walter Kluge, P.F. Kluge's father
(1903-1975)*

Towards late summer of the year of 1922, I received a letter from my Mom asking me if I wanted to go to America. Apparently Uncle Bruno had asked Mom in a letter if I was interested. Here a dream was coming true! America, the land where money was laying in the streets, and the land of the Wild West! I was to go there and I remembered all the books I had read about the Indians, the land of General Custer and Sitting Bull. Did I want to go …! I wrote to Uncle Bruno the very same night, and he, in turn, started the legal work of getting me into the promise land. Back to Hamburg and home. This then was to be my last Christmas at home.

Uncle Bruno sent me ten dollars to have on the boat coming over. He knew my inflated Mark was worth next to nothing. These ten dollars had more value than any other ten dollars I have ever owned. I went to at least ten banks in Hamburg before I changed it into German Marks. I think I got about 50,000 Marks for it. With about half of it, I got my sister a brand new baby carriage and with the rest some clothing for myself. All of it for ten dollars!

February 8, 1923

Now everything was ready. I had my shots, my passport and no money. In those days all the big ships left directly from the port of Hamburg, not like in later years from Cuxhafen, a small port at the mouth of the Elbe River. All the family was there. I remember Aunt Helene saying, "Well, this is a big ocean and sometimes these ships don't get there." And a few days later I thought she was right.

The Mount Clinton was a very small liner, about 5,000 tons, an American boat with some Germans in the crew. Like me, all my fellow travelers were immigrants, and with a few exceptions, in the ages between 20 and 30. This trip in early 1923 cannot be compared with the luxury of ocean traveling. But to us, still hungry from the war and after-war years, this was heaven. I still remember the first breakfast. On each plate was an orange, fresh rolls and eggs. These things I only remembered from way back before the war, and even then, eggs for breakfast only once or twice a year. And meat for lunch and dinner! I knew then that if America was anything like this, I would like my new home.

Of course, February was not the best month to cross the ocean, and 5,000 tons is not much on an angry sea. Starting in the North Sea, with the exception of a few days, it was a rather tough crossing. Almost everybody got seasick and I was no exception, but not for long. My cabin steward told me right away, "Don't lay down or you will never get up anymore. Go up on the deck and fight, get fresh air and eat a little all the time." This advice I followed and soon I was back in the dining room eating almost all by myself.

This trip was to be for, I think, almost 10 to 12 days but it took us 17 days. For a while it looked real bad. About seven days out of Hamburg in mid-ocean we lost an arm of our propeller. That evening I cannot forget. Each evening a small orchestra played for us in the dining room after supper. It must have been about ten o'clock or later when all of sudden the boat felt like it was going over rocks. The music stopped. I saw some pale faces getting paler. Up on deck, officers were running toward the stern. Out there in the dark a cold wind was blowing. Soon after the rocking stopped, or almost so, we had to reduce our speed to almost half. So instead of getting to the promised land on time, it took us 17 days.

The talk among my fellow travelers was mostly about where we were going, who would be waiting, what would you be doing and whether you have a job. We also had a few wise guys on board. I think every boat has one or two of them. One of them was going over for a second time and knew all about America. I told him my uncle was living on Seventh Avenue and 110th Street and was a superintendent of an apartment house. "Oh," he said, "You've got nothing to worry about. He's got a big job and you're going to live like a king!"

On the morning of February the 25th, the Mount Clinton steamed into the harbor of New York. Since early morning I was up on deck very excited, waiting to see land again after seventeen days of rough going. Out of the mist there it is, the skyscrapers and over there the Statue of Liberty! This was no dream any more. I was here and no matter what was coming, it had to be better. This was America!

In the early twenties, thousands and thousands of immigrants from all parts of the globe came to these shores each year and all of them had to enter through the offices and halls of Ellis Island. I was no exception. This place was no hotel. Here you had to strip right down to nothing and a team of doctors probed you for any defects and sickness. Also your papers had to be in order and you had to have ten dollars. These, by the way, came to me soon after we docked. I think it was Western Union who delivered them to me. I had to spend one night there and you could see happiness and real sadness. I saw families who for one reason or another had been waiting for weeks and months to be released and I spoke with some of them who already knew they had to go back. All their dreams shattered and nothing to live for.

We found this written account of my father's journey to America in an 86-page autobiography he wrote late in life. Walter Kluge did not return to Germany until 1954, on the trip I recount in the previous chapter.

WHERE I CALL HOME
Gambier's Citizen of the Year – July 4, 2015

Every year the village of Gambier chooses a Citizen of the Year. To my surprise, in 2015 it was me. My friend and classmate, Perry Lentz, did the honors.

My dear old friend:

You first returned to Gambier in 1987 as a visitor, accompanied only by your **Dog. Day, Afternoon** and evening thereafter though, your unmatched experience, your gregarious friendliness, your sense of humor and your edgy eloquence wove themselves into the fabric of this Village, and in time you brought your wonderful wife, Pamela here and established your home.

But given that you also adopted the role of the "Salman Rushdie of Knox County," the H L Menecken of College Township, I always thought that **The Day That I Die** would come before a 4th of July that would see you chosen for this particular honor. But we always have to be r-**Eddie, and the Cruisers** speed, the p-t boat speed, the jet-plane speed at which time passes can bring about extraordinary surprises.

You've always been openly disdainful toward current figures of authority and administration and the professoriate, and in your mind Denham Sutcliffe's presence looms just as dauntingly over the College today as, say, Douglas **MacArthur's Ghost** does over the

Philippines. But we puny contemporary inhabitants of this village have nonetheless come to cherish you, fascinated for example by your ongoing struggle to protect your flora against the local fauna, which makes each spring a *Season for War* at 221 Ward Street, with your chicken wire and Havahart traps and weaponized coyote urine, you seek to defend your own garden of Eden, your own *Edge of Paradise*, against woodchuck and deer and raccoon.

As acerbic as you are, your service to your *Alma Mater* has been extraordinarily valuable by any measure that it at all fair or *Final. Exam*-ining your record both here and in the Village, it is hard to know which contribution has been the *Biggest. Elvis* Presley, say or John Wayne (whom you once interviewed) or John Green (whom you once taught) have in their different spheres millions more fans, of course, but none of theirs are more intelligently and personally devoted than those fans you've won for yourself from generations of Gambier Villagers and Kenyon graduates – among them John Green, who in public appearances and national magazines always acknowledges your crucial influence upon him

Were you to be *Gone Tomorrow* from our midst, responding say to a *Call from Jersey* or from Saipan or Singapore or Semester at Sea, we'd miss you terribly, even though your sardonic commentary about us and your effective sleuthing into our secrets are those of a *Master. Blaster* though you are of all administrators younger than Tom Edwards, and of all those village or collegiate changes toward which time has inevitably compelled us, you are deeply cherished.

What I've just read incorporates the title of your article which begot one of the most famous films of all time, and also the title of every one of your books – and I know that you would want everyone here today to know that every one of those books is currently available for purchase.

My task would have been far, far easier had you written books and articles with different titles. Since your peculiar virtues are unlikely to dissipate, here are some possible titles for your future books – feel free to use them as you wish.

"This is a Country for Old Men," or *"Driving Miss Mavis."* You always treat the elderly with an old-world courtesy, with unfailing respect and genuine interest and warm good humor. And so too do you treat the very young, as witness to your warm and spontaneous inclusion of Tom Lockard's grandsons in your memorial tribute to Tom. In the matter of such memorial tributes "It is not by chance," reads a document supporting this award, "that [your] penetrating, poignant observations on individuals are often quoted in college obituaries."

Other possible titles, which I surely could have used today: *"Return of The Native Who Happens to be a Contributing Editor to National Geographic Traveler,"* or – with a nod to George Orwell – *"The Road to Wiggins Street"* or *"You Can Go Home Again (if you don't care what the folks there think of you).*" You have "the detachment and truth-telling of a travel writer," yet you are passionately attached to this place. So we often find ourselves under your gaze and under your ball-point pen. To see ourselves as others see us, others who care enough about us to give us an honest accounting, is not always comfortable, but it is always beneficial.

Other titles, which are yours for the taking: *"The Ballad of the Happy Café"* or *"The French Toast Also Rises"* or perhaps *"Plant It Again, Sam."* You have met and engaged with some of the most famous people of our culture – John Wayne and Ann-Margaret and Peter Falk and Jane Smiley – yet you have taken just as much interest in, and you have just as fully honored and celebrated, the people hereabouts who have prepared your French toast, sold you your fir trees, maintained your classrooms and did your typing.

Other possible titles: *"Plays Surprisingly Well With Others,"* or *"A Man for All Readings"*: you are always very generous in giving your time locally: to local book clubs, and to hosting off-hand, off-line, or off-*Kenyon Review* literary events. And you handle such things richly and generously, as when a Mt. Vernon lady at one of your presentations at the library said that reading *Master Blaster* made her "never ever want to go to Saipan." Your warm smile in response said it all: she was that independent, crusty, quirky, and courageous reader in whose company you delight.

Other titles I could have used: *"The Gossip Archipelago,"* or *"An Abundance of Confidences,"* or perhaps – in the fashion of *I, Robot* or *I, Claudius* – *"I, Vacuum-Cleaner."* The following statement supporting this award needs to be quoted: "He is…a public personality who adds to the liveliness and intellectual elevation of the village, at the same time that he vacuums-up information and distributes it, thereby contributing to mostly well-informed gossip." And don't we all agree that every village needs "well-informed gossip"?

And a final suggested title *"Gambier is Not a Paper Town."* You have made Gambier, Ohio as famous as Winesburg, Ohio. The crucial difference is that Sherwood Anderson's Winesburg was completely fictitious – Anderson didn't know that there really was a Winesburg, when he wrote his novel – while your Gambier is altogether real.

And today it honors you, P.F. Kluge, as its Citizen of the Year.

A READING LIST

Years ago, some students asked me a question that was at once flattering and intimidating: What should they read after they graduate? I answered promptly. I didn't fuss with genres, nationalities, publication date or popularity. I winged it. This is the list my students took out of my office, a long list but incomplete. I'm still reading. And to this first list, I have appended something else, the syllabus for a course I never taught: Dead White Males.

Nelson Algren	*Collected Stories*
Edward Allen	*Mustang Sally*
Sherwood Anderson	*Winesburg, Ohio, Poor White*
David Bradley	*The Chaneysville Incident*
William Brinkley	*The Last Ship*
Willa Cather	*My Antonia,*
	The Professor's House
Raymon Chandler	*Farewell My Lovely,*
	The Simple Art of Murder
John Cleland	*Fanny Hill*
Evan S. Connell	*Mrs. Bridge, Mr. Bridge*
Joseph Conrad	*Youth, Victory, Lord Jim*
Louis DeBernieses	*Captain Corelli's Mandolin*
Pete Dexter	*Paris Trout*
John Dos Passos	*U.S.A.*
Katherine Dunn	*Greek Love*
Esi Edugyan	*Half Blood Blues*
Tan Tuan Eng	*The Gift of Rain,*
	Garden of the Evening Mists
Hans Falkda	*Every Man Dies Alone*

Thomas Flanagan	*The Year of the French,*
	Tenants of Time,
	The End of the Hunt
Richard Ford	*The Lay of the Land,*
	The Sportswriter,
	Independence Day,
	Let Me Be Frank
Ben Fountain	*Billy Lynn's Long Halftime Walk*
Tena French	*In the Woods*
Leonard Gardner	*Fat City*
Graham Greene	*The Quiet American,*
	The Heart of the Matter,
	The Comedians,
	A Burnt-Out Case
	Film: *The Third Man*
Nikolai Gogol	*Dead Souls*
Mashing Hamid	*The Reluctant Fundamentalist,*
	How to Get Rich in Rising Asia
Thomas Kelly	*The Rackets, Empire Rising*
John Lancaster	*The Debt to Pleasure*
Ring Lardner	*Collected Short Stories*
	"The Gold Honeymoon"
D.H. Lawrence	*The Shop of Death* (Poem),
	Lady Chatterly's Lover,
	The Rainbow
John LeCarre	*The Spy Who Came In From The Cold*
Harper Lee	*To Kill A Mockingbird*
Yiyun Li	*The Vagrants,*
	A Thousand Years of Good Prayers
Andre Malraux	*Man's Fate*
Michael Malone	*Handling Sin*
Thomas Mann	*Death in Venice,*
	The Magic Mountain,
	Confessions of Felix Krull,
	Confidence Man
Peter Matthiesen	*At Play in the Fields of the Lord*
Alice McDermott	*Charming Billy, That Night*

H.L. Mencken	Essays: *"In Memoriam W.J.B.",* *"Chiropractic"*
A.D. Miller	*Snowdrops*
Susannah More	*In the Cut*
Vladimir Nabokov	*Lolita*
Tim O'Brien	*The Things They Carried*
George Orwell	Essays *"Politics and the English Language", 1984, Animal Farm, Coming Up for Air*
George Pelecanos	*Drama City, The Midnight Gardener, The Cut*
Philip Roth	*Portnoy's Complaint, American Pastoral, Nemesis*
Paul Scott	*Staying On*
Neville Shute	*On the Beach*
Colm Toibin	*The Master*
Leo Tolstoy	*War and Peace, Anna Karenina, The Death of Ivan Ilyich*
Ivan Turgenev	*First Love, A Sportsman's Sketches*
John Updike	*Rabbit Run, Rabbit Redux, Rabbit is Rich, Rabbit at Rest*
Edith Wharton	*The Age of Innocence*
Colson Whitehead	*Zone One*
Timothy Weiner	*Enemies, Legacy of Ashes*
John Williams	*Stoner, Butchers Crossing*
Austin Wright	*Tony and Susan*

This is a commanding list of important books. But I confess the pleasure I take when I scan a rack of books at an airport or in a supermarket and select a book I've never heard of. It might please or disappoint. You never know.

This additional list I labeled DWM, Dead White Males.
Before it's too late: say hello to this vanishing bunch!

They grow up, (sort of)	*Portnoy's Complaint*
They leave home	*The Last Picture Show*
They go into business	*Babbitt*
They follow sports	*A Fan's Notes*
They sell American cars!	*Appointment In Samarra*
They sell Japanese cars!	*Rabbit is Rich*
They get divorced	*Cathedral*
They shoot drugs	*Man With A Golden Arm*
They chase women	*Bright Lights, Big City*
They chase girls	*Lolita*
They lost a war	*A Flag For Sunrise*
They go into politics	*All The King's Men*
They move to Florida and die	*Continental Drift*

ONE LAST THING
Commencement for the Class of 2020

Honorary Degree for P.F. Kluge, written and read at commencement by Wendy MacLeod, James Michael Playwright-in-Residence.

Litterarum Humaniorum Doctoris

The son of German immigrants, you came to the Hill when it was a college of 400 students. You played hardball on your application, telling Kenyon that: "my first choice is the college from which I get a scholarship."

You became editor-in-chief of *The Collegian* where you advocated for the "radical change" that led to women coming to Kenyon. You graduated summa cum laude, Phi Beta Kappa, with Highest Honors in English and went on to get a doctorate with distinction from the University of Chicago. A natural teacher, you reflexively graded everything – from speeches to administrative responses.

You told John Green that his best stories were the ones he told on breaks and he credits you for making him a writer. You wrote the *LIFE* magazine article that became *Dog Day Afternoon*, which gave you a perpetual Hollywood patina, Mr. Chips as played by William Holden. *Alma Mater*, your love letter to Kenyon, demonstrated your ability to be both fond and clear-eyed. Called a "seasoned ironist" by *The New York Times*, you are a model of productivity – writing memoirs, novels, travel articles and murder mysteries – all while cultivating students who became your pals, acolytes, and adopted children.

You're a campus character in the best sense of the word, the only faculty member to be honored with both Citizen of the Year and a bespoke cocktail at The Alcove. We wish you and Pamela continued adventures and a beautiful garden.

Printed in the USA
CPSIA information can be obtained
at www.ICGtesting.com
LVHW071347070224
771185LV00079B/2498